D1713461

Observations on the Ethnology of the Sauk Indians

BY

Alanson Skinner

GREENWOOD PRESS, PUBLISHERS
WESTPORT, CONNECTICUT

Originally published in 1923-1925
by order of the Board of Trustees,
Milwaukee Public Museum, Milwaukee, Wisconsin

Reprinted with the permission
of the Milwaukee Public Museum

First Greenwood Reprinting 1970

Library of Congress Catalogue Card Number 79-111400

SBN 8371-4632-1

Printed in the United States of America

BULLETIN

OF THE

PUBLIC MUSEUM OF THE CITY OF MILWAUKEE

Vol. 5, No. 1, pp. 1-57, plate 1   August 30, 1923

Observations on the Ethnology of the Sauk Indians

BY

Alanson Skinner

OBSERVATIONS ON THE ETHNOLOGY OF THE SAUK INDIANS

CONTENTS

PHONETIC KEY

The phonetics employed in recording the native names and terms found in this and the succeeding papers of this series are as follows:

ä, as in flat	sh, as in short
â, as aw in raw	º, a whispered final vowel
ê, as in pen	ᵘ, a whispered final vowel
î, as in pin	', a glottal stop
û, as in mud	x, an aspirant

The other letters used have the usual values assigned them in English.

INTRODUCTION

The following notes were obtained while making a collection of specimens, representing the material culture of the Sauk Indians for the Public Museum of the City of Milwaukee during the months of May, June and July, 1922. They are by no means complete, yet serve to illustrate the specimens gathered, and are published principally because of the great paucity of material descriptive of the life and customs of this important Central Algonkian tribe, and as a part of the writer's studies on the Central Algonkian and Southern Siouan groups. A good bibliography of the subject may be found under Sauk in the Handbook of American Indians.[1] This includes many of the older authorities. The accompanying article by J. N. Hewitt also embodies many facts of interest.

The Indian informant, from whom most of the information concerning customs of the Sauk was gathered, is the writer's interpreter and field assistant, the Rev. Wm. Harris or Mê'siwûk, ("Tree-without-limbs" or "Tree-stripped-of-limbs"). He is a Sauk of the Bear gens, and a nephew of the Chief Keokuk. Up until a few years ago, he was a "pagan" member of Mokoho'ko's Band, but is now a convert to Christianity and Pastor of "The Only Way" Baptist Church near Avery, Oklahoma. Mr. Harris was born 77 years ago in Kansas, and is well informed upon the rites of his people, having been brought up in a conservative family. Mr. Harris is a member of the Oskû'sh moiety, and was long an attendant or waiter at the meetings of the Medicine Lodge Fraternity, although not actually a member. In consequence he is well posted as to the beliefs of the society, although naturally not so deeply acquainted with the mysteries as one of the leaders.

Additional material, especially on the rites of the Medicine Lodge, was given by one of the chief priests or masters named "Frank Smith," who resides near Shawnee, Oklahoma, and from whom several ceremonial articles, among them a number of animal skin medicine bags of considerable antiquity were obtained. Some further data were added by

---

[1]Bur. Amer. Ethn., Bull. 30, vol. 2, 1910.

Ki'shämäk^w, of the Kwa'skwami Band, located near Reserve, Kansas, on what was the Great Nemaha Reservation. Still further information was obtained from Sisi'a or Aveline Givens, Harding Franklin, and Jesse James, all of Cushing, Oklahoma.

FORMER HISTORY OF THE SAUK

The traditional home of the Sauk was probably the region about Saginaw Bay in the eastern peninsula of Michigan, whence they were expelled in late prehistoric times—that is, shortly prior to the coming of the first whites into their country. Algonkian tradition about the Great Lakes states that the expulsion of the Sauk was at the hands of the Ojibway. It is possible that, as Hewitt declares, the Iroquoian Neutrals had something to do with their flight, but all historic references to the antagonists of the Neutrals seem to refer distinctly to the Potawatomi,[2] or to the Mascoutens.[3]

In their retreat from the Ojibway, the Sauk fled across Lake Michigan, probably via Mackinaw straits, and, continuing southward, settled, according to Menomini tradition, on what is now the Door County peninsula, the long northward pointing arm of land which forms the east coast of Green Bay, Wisconsin. Here, directly opposite the Menomini headquarters, they found asylum for a time. However, their aggressive and warlike nature soon brought them into violent conflict with the peaceful Menomini, who, although probably fewer in numbers, and far less martial by nature, after a war of varying fortunes, eventually forced the withdrawal of the Sauk from the peninsula to the lands along the Fox river, from its mouth southward, where they were found by Father Allouez in 1667.

With the coming of the French, the Sauk and their allies, the Foxes, proved to be the only Algonkian peoples who were on an unfriendly footing with the newcomers. Bitter fighting ensued, in which the Sauk and Fox again suffered defeat at the hands of the Menomini, now allied with the Winnebago and the French. The Iroquois, too, were called into service against them by the whites, and for a long time an entire village made up of captive Fox, or more properly "Mûskwaki'," was colonized among the Iroquois in western New York, the locality being

---

[2] They are referred to as the "Fire Nation" which is an exact translation of the word Potawatomi.

[3] The term Mascoutens signifies "Little Prairie" and seems to indicate that even at that early date the Potawatomi were divided into the groups which still exist and which we now recognize as "Forest" and "Prairie" bands.

known today as "Skwaki Hill." A number of Seneca still claim descent from the "Skwakihows," and the Muskwaki of Tama, Iowa, are said to preserve traditions of their relationship to the Iroquois. It is possible that certain Iroquois customs, such as the torture of prisoners, may have been thus introduced to the Fox and so to the Sauk. At all events the surrounding Algonkian tribes declare that it was not their custom to torture captives until the Sauk began to do so.

The Sauk were gradually thrust southward and westward by the power of their enemies, the final act in the drama being the Black Hawk war. Although there can be little doubt but that Black Hawk, deserted by Keokuk, and betrayed by his Winnebago and Potawatomi allies, would have been defeated by American troops in the long run, the massacre of a party of defenseless Menomini at their camp on an island in the Mississippi near Prairie du Chien, Wisconsin, precipitated the end. While there seems to be justification for this attack by the Sauk on the Menomini, for there are records that some Eastern Sioux and Menomini had murdered a party of Sauk warriors the year before, it was ill-timed. Menomini tradition, which seems well substantiated by contemporary historical data, says that runners were at once dispatched to all their important settlements, the partisans took down their sacred war-bundles, and the tribe, hitherto neutral, sent out all its available warriors, some with the American troops, others under their own leaders. Simultaneously the "Santee" Dakota, with whom the Menomini held a long and cherished friendship, were also called upon for help by the latter, and, incidentally, by the white authorities. Black Hawk, who had hitherto waged war with some success, was rapidly overwhelmed, and finally all the Sauk followed the pioneers of the tribe westward across the Mississippi, never to return.

The change in environment from the shores of the Great Lakes to the plains was indeed a profound one, but no more so than the accompanying change of culture must have been. On the lake shore the Sauk were fishers and followers of the inland sea. They were expert canoemen, and great utilizers of birch bark. One of their ancient gentes is named Kêtcikûmi, or the Great Sea, a term applied both to Lake Superior and Lake Michigan by the Woodland Algonkians. Their traditions are replete with allusions to a maritime existence, for their old lake shore life was no less, as can be appreciated by those only who have examined the wind-swept sand dune archeological sites of the tribes dwelling along these lakes.

On the borders of the plains they came in contact with the buffalo and peoples of a buffalo-hunting culture. Buffalo hide took the place of bark, though in some cases the forms of the utensils which they made, for example, the rawhide trunks, remained the same. The bull boat supplanted the canoe, and the buffalo hunt the gathering of wild rice. Some of their buffalo hunts led the Sauk even beyond the border of Colorado.

Whereas the Sauk had formerly associated chiefly with the Central Algonkian Menomini and Potawatomi, the northern Algonkian Ojibway, and the Siouan Winnebago; they were now in active contact with the Ioway, Oto, and Osage, of southern Siouan stock. The culture of these tribes, while closest to the Central Algonkian in point of things material, differs strongly on the side of mental, social, and religious activities, and it is probably from these peoples, especially from the Ioway who befriended and fraternized with them, that the peculiarly complex and unusually stiff gens organization of the Sauk, so unlike the indefinite and loose customs of the general run of Algonkians of the central region, is due, although Iroquoian influence may have played some part.

The Sauk evidently made no little impression on the inhabitants, both red and white, in the territories through which they passed. In Wisconsin, in particular, there may still be found numerous names derived from that of the tribe, among them Ozaukee County, Sauk County, Prairie du Sac, and Saukville.

This very brief and incomplete account of Sauk history takes little notice of the Fox, who are now wholly separated from their old allies, and are situated at Tama, Iowa. They seem to be more distinct from the Sauk in all matters save material culture than has been generally realized, and should be considered separately by ethnologists. The Sauk feel keenly that they are a distinct tribe, as much so as the Kickapoo or even the Potawatomi. It may well be that even in material culture the Fox are farther removed from the Sauk than is now supposed. At present the Fox are by far the more conservative group of the two.

Unlike the Tama Fox, or Mûskwaki', the Sauk of Oklahoma dwell almost entirely in modern frame houses with many conveniences. The finding of oil on Sauk lands in recent years has made them well-to-do, and the automobile, player piano, victrola, and other luxuries are seen everywhere. Yet the Sauk are still conservative in the matter of religion, for in the rear of many of the houses may be seen rectangular bark lodges in which still hang the gens sacred bundles and in whose shelter ancient rites are still carried on. In not a few instances, the older members of the family dwell in these houses, or in the round mat wigwams used in winter in earlier days. Small lodges for the housing of women undergoing their menses are still frequent adjuncts to modern dwellings, and bough arbors or shelters abound.

Even in cases where all members of the family are users of the narcotic peyote and are members of its religious cult, the people seem to cling to the beliefs and relics of the past at heart, and are no more willing to sell their sacred objects than are the professing pagans. In fact, of recent years, the users of peyote seem to have, in a measure, reconciled or adjusted the old beliefs to the new, and do not seem so anxious to discard the paraphernalia of "paganism" as they were a few years ago.

The Sauk, according to the Handbook of American Indians, formerly numbered about 3500 souls. In 1909 there were 536 Sauk in Oklahoma and 87 in Kansas. At this time the Muskwaki were recorded as 352, all, or nearly all, at Tama, Iowa. It is thought that the Muskwaki probably once numbered about 3000. The period of greatest population of both tribes was probably about 1650, when they first encountered the whites.

The name "Sauk" is variously translated. The sign used in the sign language means "something sprouting up," which is frequently given as the meaning of the name. However, the more popular translation is "Yellow Earth" as opposed to "Red Earth," the proper name of the Muskwaki or Fox. Some even say that in former times the Sauk painted in yellow ochre and the Fox in red, just as the moieties of the Sauk today paint in black and white. The translation "Yellow Earth,"[3a] agrees with the explanation given by the Menomini and other of their Algonkian neighbors.

In the sign language the Muskwaki are designated by the signs for red, earth, and painting oneself. The related Kickapoo are indicated by a sign meaning "straight cut hair."

[3a]The translation "Yellow Earth" has long been known, and is probably correct. W. P. Clark, author of "The Indian Sign Language, Phila., 1885," on page 323, says that Keokuk (probably Moses, son of the well known chief) told him that, "God made the Sacs out of yellow, and the Foxes out of red, earth." At that time also the sign for Sauk was simply "shaved head." The idea of "something sprouting up" seems to be a very modern "folk explanation."

SOCIAL AND POLITICAL ORGANIZATION

Inasmuch as the earlier writers, and indeed most of those of later times, have failed to realize that the Sauk and Fox are two separate and distinct peoples, it is impossible to utilize much of the information which may be found scattered throughout American ethnological literature because of the confusion of data.[4] Thus Lewis H. Morgan gives a list of Sauk and Fox gentes, but, as he does not distinguish between the two tribes it is unavailable here.

J. N. B. Hewitt, writing in the Handbook of American Indians under the caption of "Sauk" on uncredited authority, probably the late Dr. William Jones, gives us no less than fourteen gentes. Of this number, however, my principal informant among the Oklahoma Sauk, Mê′siwûk, or the Reverend Wm. Harris, himself long an officer of the Bear gens, and in this capacity frequently called upon to give names in not only his own gens, but in those gentes with which his enjoyed reciprocal functions, was unable to identify six; namely, the Trout, Sturgeon, Bass, Great Lynx or Fire Dragon, Swan, and Grouse. Harris is of the opinion that all of these names are personal titles in the Fish, Great Sea, and perhaps Thunder gentes. Certainly all but two, Trout and Grouse, occur in the lists of gens names which Harris furnished. Undoubtedly Trout is a Fish gens name. If, as the writer suspects, Hewitt derived his information from Jones, who was a Fox by descent, it is quite probable that the data is colored by Dr. Jones' superior knowledge of Fox ethnology, which led him to infer identity of thought and custom for the Sauk many times where this was not the case, as for example, in the account given in the Handbook of the attitude of the Sauk toward their former chiefs Keokuk and Black Hawk, which, according to the statements of the present day Indians, is incorrect.

Marston[5] gives twelve Sauk gentes of which the Sturgeon, Perch,

---

[4]The following data furnished by Dr. Truman Michelson are of interest as bearing on this question:
"Apropos of Sauk and Fox, in Elsie C. Parsons' American Indian Life, p. 386: "though they are, even today, distinct in language, ethnology, and mythology." And in the Journal of the Washington Academy of Sciences, Vol. LX, p. 492, in speaking of the Foxes at Tama: "in language they are Foxes; also in ethnology . . . . . the much heralded amalgamation with the Sauks is shown to be a myth." On the Sauk population see p. 490, et sq. I there show that certain large figures are mere fabrications. The paper I spoke of in Milwaukee is "Some general notes on the Fox Indians." It is in the above Journal, Vol. IX, p. 483, et sq., 521 et sq., 593 et sq. You will find there many documentary references to the Sauks and Foxes that are apparently unknown to most ethnologists. Some of these I previously pointed out in my review of Mary Owen's Folk Lore of the Musquakie Indians of North America (Current Anthropological Literature, Vol. II, p. 233 et sq.)"
[5]E. H. Blair's "Indian Tribes of the Upper Mississippi and the Great Lakes Region," Cleveland, 1911, pp. 190-191.

Black Bass, Swan, and Panther are probably gens personal names.

In addition to the gentes, the Sauk tribe is divided into two moieties which are wholly independent of the gentes, and also, in former years it was further subdivided into several local bands, again quite regardless of gens or moiety, members of both moieties and any or all gentes being found in each. These bands are now obsolete.

BANDS

The bands into which the Sauk were formerly divided took their names or nicknames from their chiefs or from some real or fancied personal peculiarities. They were:

1. *Pä'thihuk,* or "Poker Players." This was Keokuk's band.
2. *Wishâ'tahuk,* or "Sweaty People." This was Gray Eyes' band.
3. *Wishigê'shihuk,* or "Strong Band." This was Mokohoko's band.
4. *A'ˣkanûk,* "Bone" or "Skeleton" band, so-called because wasted by smallpox.
5. *Tci'kwoskûk,* "Walks-on-the-bank's-edge's" band, so-called from their leader, a Muskwaki chief of the Deer gens who deserted his own people to live with the Sauk.

6 and 7 should no doubt be *Kwa'skwami's* and Black Hawk's bands. The latter is largely exterminated, but the survivors of the former still reside at Nemaha, Neb.

MOIETIES

With the Sauk, membership in either of the two tribal moieties depends on the sequence of birth of the individual. In other words, the first born goes to the opposite moiety from that of the father, the second into the father's moiety, and so on, in alternate rotation. Thus, if a father is Ki'shko (the moiety using white paint) his eldest son will be Oskû'sh (black paint) and the next Ki'shko, etc., sex making no difference, except that, in some instances at least, a girl seems to be taken into the moiety of her eldest brother.

Ki'shko and Oskû'sh do not divide and oppose each other for dances and ceremonies, as is popularly supposed—the eating contest at adoptions and other functions excepted—but always do so for games.

The eating contest above mentioned is an hilarious affair. Four young men are selected from each moiety, and a bowl of boiling hot stewed dog, cooked very tender, is set between them, the meat being cut into eight pieces. At the east end of the lodge a war spear is thrust upright in the ground.

At a given signal, the Oskû′sh, as is their right, grab first into the boiling mess, while the Ki′shko follow, gobbling to see who can swallow all of his boiling portion first. He who wins, springs up, if able, with a whoop, runs as fast as nature will permit to the upright lance, and rubs it up and down with his greasy hands, exclaiming: "This is what I′ll do when I go to war!" meaning he will slay an enemy.

According to tradition, an Oskû′sh must complete anything he undertakes, but a Ki′shko may give up or turn back. A lone member of one moiety amid a group of the opposite class is liable to much teasing and good natured banter, as has come under my personal observation.

GENTES

1. Bear, called *Mû′kwa* or *Makwî′sûjîk.*
2. Buffalo, called *Nänoso′skwajîk,* "Those who have Buffalo Division."
3. Wolf, *Mahwä′sujîk.*
4. Fox, *Wagushe′siwîk.*
5. Fish, *Pakahamouwä′sujîk,* "Tight Bodied People."
6. Thunder, *Wämegoiwisujîk* or *Ninäme′ˣkiwûk.*
7. Eagle, *Kêtiwî′sojîk.*
8. Great Sea (Lake Michigan?), *Kêtcikûmi.*
9. Beaver, *Oma′kwê′sojîk.*
10. Deer, *Pêshigishiwî′sojîki.*
11. Indian Potato, *Päniwesojîk* or *Mûkopä′niäk,* Bear Potato.
12. Turkey, *Penäwä′sujîk.*
13. Elk, identity now probably lost. The gens is amalgamated with the deer.

RECIPROCAL FUNCTIONS OF GENTES

The gentes as enumerated below in the first column call upon those given in the second column to furnish waiters for all gens functions, and vice versa.

Host Gens	Serving Gens
1. Bear	Buffalo, Deer, Potato, Sea, Elk
2. Buffalo	Bear, Turkey

WAITER'S INVITING TERMS

When messengers or waiters are sent from one gens to another with the invitations to a feast, they do not address the members of the gens by their ordinarily accepted title, but by a ceremonial term, some of which are as follows:

1. Bear Gens, *Kishkîtihuk*, Short Tails.
2. Buffalo Gens, *Wäwiwi'nitcîk*, Those Who Have Horns.
3. Wolf Gens, *Papamitcikwä'huk*, Those Who Run with Head Sideways.
4. Fox Gens, *Apahî'kûnûnwikûtajîk*, Those Who Like to Eat Buckskin Scraps.
5. Fish Gens, *Nä'mäwûk*, Sturgeons.
6. Thunder Gens, *Wämegwûnämähûk*, You Who Have Feathers.
7. Eagle Gens, (?).
8. Great Sea Gens, *Wisupiage'tuhûk*, Moving Water People.
9. Beaver Gens, *Kishkikû'tcäkähûk*, Root Biters.
10. Deer Gens, *Wapîskanua'jîk*, The White Tailed Gens.
11. Bear-Potato, *Kiwa'piajîk*, Those Who Vine Out.
12. Turkey Gens, *Pêmikûnäbâhûk*, Roosters Above.

In inviting any given gens to attend a feast or ceremony, the waiter gives the chief of that gens one of his invitation sticks, and the chief, on accepting it asks, "Who do you want?" whereupon the waiter replies, using one of the terms given above, adding the information as to the place and time of the function.

Members of gentes bearing reciprocal ceremonial functions towards each other often address each other, as "My Waiter." For instance,

I have heard a Sauk of the Bear gens call to a member of the Deer gens as we were passing, "Hello, my Waiter."

GENS TABUS AND CUSTOMS

If a wolf barked at a Wolf gens member from the east, it was a sign that someone of his family would soon die.

Mr. Harris is of the opinion that in former times the chieftainship of the Sauk tribe was hereditary in the Fish gens, but in more recent years minor chiefs at least have been elected from among the warriors of the Thunder gens.

ADOPTION INTO ANOTHER GENS

Sometimes a woman will have her child adopted into her gens instead of allowing it to go to the father's gens as usual. This is done by giving a feast to the father's gens, at which time formal announcement of the adoption is made.

An example of this cross gens adoption is that of Frank Smith, whose father was Wa'pikahân or "White Bear's Fat" of the Bear gens. Frank was adopted into the Thunder gens on behalf of his mother, Pemiwa'käkᵂ, or "Moulting Feathers," and at that time was named Pi'ätcisât, or "Flying Over."

Sometimes a person who is adopted to fill the place of the dead is also taken over into the opposite moiety from that to which he formerly belonged.

ADOPTION CEREMONY

When a person dies, the moiety brothers of the deceased "clean the grave of grass and weeds" at intervals, and, after a month has elapsed, a feast is given by the family of the deceased and a person adopted to fill the place of the departed.

An old man is elected to take charge and erect a "war post." The guest of honor, the candidate for adoption, is dressed in fine clothes at the expense of the mourners. He is then seated in state by himself. When all is in readiness, the male members of the two moieties, Oskû'sh and Ki'shko, vie with east other in counting coups—or, as Wm. Harris said, "telling how many scalps they had brought home to their uncles," Oskû'sh going first, as is customary, and Ki'shko following.

As each warrior counts coup—that is, relates the time, place, and circumstances of his deed, he strikes the war post, and all present cry "Hau!"

After the contest is over, there is the usual eating contest and general feast, after which the candidate goes about the circle and gives presents of calicoes and blankets to the warriors, and they in turn present these to their sisters or nieces. It is a breech of etiquette to retain the presents or take them home.

The ceremony is now ended, and from that time on the candidate takes the place of the deceased in the family of mourners.

NAMING CUSTOMS

Every Sauk child inherits an ordinal name at birth, as is the custom among many other tribes, such as the Menomini, Ioway, and Dakota. These names are as follows, beginning with the first born:

Boys	Girls
Mûdji'kiwîs	*Kê'tcikwäo*
A'nêkutc	*Nishonêmêkikwäo*
Näso'nomûk	*Nyä'konomêk*
Yâo'nänûk	*Okoêtci'a*
Akoêtci'ª	

As previously stated, the eldest child belongs in the opposite moiety from its father. Thus, if the father is Oskû'sh, the first born is mudji'-kiwîs or Kê'tcikwäo, as the sex determines, and of the Ki'shko moiety. However, at adoptions to take the place of the dead, a child or an adult may be taken over into the opposite moiety.

When the child is from ten to thirty days of age, its parents and relatives give a dog feast at which its father's moiety in particular appears in force. As usual, before the others are served, the waiters set before four men from each moiety, kettles of boiling dog meat, cut in equal portions. This hot food the contestants gobble down, each trying to outdo the rest.

After this, an old man of the father's gens, to whom this part of the ceremony has been intrusted, rises and announces the name which he has decided to confer upon the child, and the moiety to which the baby will belong. He then addresses a prayer to the Great Spirit, telling him what name has been conferred upon the child, and its moiety, so that it will always be recognized.

The child keeps this name until well grown, when, in the case of males, it is likely to be changed as a reward for prowess on the warpath. If a warrior is among the first four to touch the body of a slain enemy, his name is discarded and a new name is at once given him by the partisan in charge of the war party. This becomes his title without further ceremony. It may be that a particularly successful brave may have his name changed several times in the course of his life, depending on his ability in battle.

One rule that is strictly observed, both in the naming of children, and in the subsequent changing of names as war honors, is that the name must have some reference to the gens eponym. This may be by directly naming the animal, or by reference to some habit, attribute, characteristic, or quality, either real or mythical, of the animal, or even by reference to some associated animal or article.

The writer was unable to determine that these names were set, and handed down from generation to generation by the Sauk as is the case among their relatives, the Menomini. Among the latter the gens names were accorded as great honors, were limited in numbers, and could only be held by one incumbent during a lifetime. With the Sauk the number seems unlimited, and the impression given was that new gens names could be coined whenever occasion demanded, although it is quite probable that many times sons succeeded to their father's titles, and possibly names were also sometimes changed on the occasion of ceremonial adoptions.

ASSUMING A NEW NAME BECAUSE OF WAR EXPLOITS

As above noted it was customary for Sauk warriors who had accomplished some brave deed in war to "throw away" their old names and assume or be given new ones in commemoration of the event. Mê'siwûk told of the following incident in which the new names were not generally accepted by the tribe, and the men who had counted "coup" in so tame a manner were generally jeered at by the people.[6]

"Once, about 1871, a Sauk named Piätwä'tûk (Coming Sound, a Thunder gens name) lost all his horses by theft, and accused the Pawnee. I was living with my uncle, Chief Keokuk, and was one of

---

[6]It is interesting to note that my Wahpeton Dakota assistant and friend Mr. Amos Oneroad declares that the Dakota would have considered a technical coup counted on a foeman as in this instance, by shaking hands, as perfectly valid, and tells me that several instances of this are still recounted by both Teton and Santee Dakota.

those called upon to help avenge the loss. They said to me, 'Come and help us, we are going for Pawnee scalps, make fifty bullets.' I went quietly about it, telling no one, and cast fifty bullets. I got my horse ready and tied him, but, as I hadn't any saddle, I went over to borrow Charlie Keokuk's saddle from the old man. When I got there and asked for it, he seemed to know already what we were going to do. 'Don't go, nephew, those Pawnee are innocent. Those fellows will only play Hell,' he said to me. So I stayed at home.

"The rest of the war party gathered that night at a lone oak tree on the prairie. The partisan was an old fellow named Ni'shkäkât or Strutting Turkey from the Turkey gens, whom the white people called Jefferson Davis. He was the one who carried the war bundle. They started out, and when close to where Pawnee City now is, they found an old Pawnee man and two women digging bugoskʷ or Indian turnips. Strutting Turkey ordered his warriors not to kill them, so instead they all rode up and shook hands with them and returned, after changing their names because they had touched the enemy. The rest of our tribe was disgusted and refused to accept the new names. They only made fun of the warriors that took them, so it is just as well that I did not go after all."

In the section following are given a number of series of personal names found in the various gentes, furnished by Rev. Wm. Harris.

It is to be noted that several of the Sauk gentes are either extinct, or nearly so, notably the Fox, Potato, and Elk gentes. In some of these cases the gens names seem to have been taken over more or less bodily into another gens closely related to the dying one. Thus Elk gens names are, to some extent, incorporated with those of the Deer gens, and Fox names with Wolf names. In other cases the names are interchangeable to a certain degree, or else duplicated in, "related" gentes. For example, the name Black Hawk, while here enumerated as the property of the Eagle gens, is also found among the Thunderers. Gourd Rattle occurs alike in the Buffalo and Great Sea gentes.

In the accompanying list the writer has marked with an asterisk each name, the equivalent of which is found among the related Menomini, but the mere occurrence of the same name among both tribes by no means infers identity. A warrior's title in one may turn up as a woman's name in the other. In fact, this is actually the case in some instances. Moreover, a name definitely identified with a gens in one tribe is likely to have no such significance in the other.

It is interesting to note that, with the exception of the Thunder gens, the gentes of the Menomini are equipped with very few names. A small number formerly did occur in each of the other divisions, but these were, both in number and character, insignificant as compared with those of the Sauk. Among the Menomini, gens names were conferred as honorary titles only upon such members of the gens as had achieved especial distinction and were supposed to be kept constantly filled, but it was not permissible for more than one man to bear any given name at any one time. That is, for example, there might not be more than one man bearing the distinguished title of "Terrible Wolf" at any given time, and he had to be a member of the Wolf gens who had earned the right to the name in battle. Such titles were apparently conferred upon warriors after their return from the warpath by act of their gens council, and not given in the field by the partisan as was the case among the Sauk.

Among the Sauk the names belonging to each gens seemed to have been unlimited in number, and new ones appear to have been frequently coined for successful warriors, who assumed them on their return from warpaths.

While the Sauk state that all their names had reference to, and were in a sense the property of, the gens of the bearer, Menomini names in general were not of this nature. The writer has before him an extensive series of Menomini names which form part of a study of the nomenclature of the Central tribes which he is preparing. Although it is yet too early for a final statement, the following general observations may be of interest.

Besides the limited number of honorary titles belonging to the Menomini gentes, there are also several very much coveted appellations bestowed upon warriors of distinction which were apparently given quite without reference to gens affiliation.

Many names were given to the bearers by their parents and refer to the dreams or supernatural experiences of the latter. Others again refer to the time of day that the child was born, the appearance of the sky at the time, or to some person or animal, natural, supernatural, or even mythological, with whom the parents of the bearer had some unusual experience. Again others derived their names from their own dream guardians, or even from personal peculiarities or habits. Some again are of the nature of nicknames. The reason for the unusual number of real gens names in the Thunder gens, is twofold, first, the Menomini visualize the Thunderbirds as members of a family each of whom possesses a name; second, many Menomini believe themselves to be reincarnated Thunderbirds, and therefore entitled to the names that they bore during their previous existence as Thunderbirds.

However, it appears that the concept of gens names is as a whole foreign to the various tribes of Algonkian stock, being found along with the entire complex of definite gens or clan organization among such peoples as have been in contact with nations of more intensive culture, as the Iroquois on the east, who have imposed much of their social organization as well as material culture upon the Delaware, Mahikan, and Mississauga for example, and the Southern Siouan on the west, the Sauk and the Fox, for instance, having been unquestionably greatly modified by the Winnebago and the Ioway. The lack of many of the well developed features of the gens and moiety among the Menomini postulates that the culture of the latter is more nearly archaic Algonkian, for the ancient tribes of that stock, as represented today by the northern Cree, Naskapi, Montagnais, and Ojibway, are of nonintensive culture, with the individual or the family as the important social unit, and the gens or clan weak or lacking.

The whole subject of Indian nomenclature is too little known, and herein lies an important and neglected study for the linguist and the ethnologist alike. The writer ventures the prophecy that there are not only tribal but group patterns, i. e., that among the component tribes of a given culture area, the same similarity of names as of other features of the local cultural complex will be noted.

Thus among the Southern Siouans one may venture to state that the type in which a name is composed of a noun modified by an adverb, as Standing Buffalo, Walking Turtle, Walking Rain, etc., will prove far more common than among the Central Algonkians. Certain names will probably prove to be popular everywhere, and will not be circumscribed by area. In the Central Algonkian-Southern Siouan group these will include such titles as: White Thunder, Red Cloud, Black Hawk, and the like.

GENS NAMES

BEAR GENS NAMES

1. *Mê'siwûk*, Tree Without Limbs, i. e., broken off by a bear climbing.[7].

---

[7]The name of my principal informant, the Rev. Wm. Harris.

2. *Wako'me*, Shoulder Shining, i. e., where licked by a bear.
3. *Koˣsêkwä*, Heavy Weight Woman, referring to the weight of a back pack of bear meat.
4. *Kagonwi'käshäo,* Long Claws, i. e., grizzly bear.
5. *Pishagâ,* Bear hide.
6. *Päshito*, Old man, also used as a term of address to a bear before killing.
7. *Pushito'nikʷ*, Winking Bear.⁸
8. *Wapiku'naiyä°*, Gray Blanket, reference to fur of grizzly bear.
9. *Kishkitiᵘ*, Bob Tail.
10. *Wapika'käᵒ*, White Spotted Breast.
11. *Tû'sihâ*, Already There (Mythical Reference).
12. *Mumagû'nâsît*, Big Feet.
13. *Kêtci'kash*, Great Claws.
14. *Wa'bano*, Dawn (Bears hide at daylight)
15. *Kêtciwabano*, Great Dawn.
16. *Wabû'nosäᵒ*, Walks Until Dawn Woman.
17. *O'winîm*, Fat (meat).
18. *Bäskutcikäo*, Bear Cracking Plums.
19. *Mûkwûmuêtc*, Bear Excrement.
20. *Mûkwi'pûshitu*, Old Man Bear.
21. *Mûkwikwi'esäᵒ*, Bear Boy.
22. *Mûko'*, Bear Cub.
23. *Shämätuk*, Hanging Lip.
24. *Seˣko'aga*, Foaming Jaws.
25. *Ma'misäsha*, Fuzzy Ear.
26. *Mâkwimê'tämu*, Bear Old Woman.
27. *Mâkwipä'shito*, Bear Old Man. (See No. 20.)
28. *Wapêna'kenak*, Scratching Bark on Tree.⁹
29. *Käku'mu*, Marks the Tree.⁹
30. *Amo'kä*, Bee Hunter.
31. *Pitci'näkât*, Pawing Honey Out.
32. *Kaki'tiyäpiᵘ*, Imprint of Buttocks on Sand.
33. *Wishäpiᵘ*, Sits Tight in Hollow Tree.
34. *Pamikâ'shîkʷ*, See His Tracks Going On.
35. *Sisu'a*, Fat, Cracklings.
36. *Makwo'winêm*, Bear Fat.

⁸Old Eye; Michelson.
⁹These two names have reference to the custom of male bears in marking the bark of trees with their claws as high as they can reach. The Sauk say this occurs in July.

37. *Makwo'uias,* Bear Meat.
38. *Nasha'kwisa^w,* Slides (backwards) Down Tree.
39. *Pêna'si^u,* Climbing Down.
40. *Nahäsi^u,* National Meat, or Everybody's Meat.
41. *Namû'sut,* Erect Standing Man.
42. *Päkutcä'piu,* Sitting Rabbit.
43. *Kishkâ'tägît,* Small Bodied Bear.
44. *Mäshänäo,* Cross Bear.
45. *Mätä'näni,* Medicine Lodge Man.
46. *Wapima'k^w,* White Bear.
47. *Wipê'kwi^w,* Wallows in Dust.
48. *Ako'nîk^w,* Snow on Back.
49. *Kêkitaku'nûmuk,* Bear Hugging Tree.
50. *Okima'kwä°,* Chief Woman.
51. *Makwîskwä'sá,* Young Woman Bear.
52. *Kwäkwänipi'kwä°,* Twinkling Eyes.
53. *Nämûswi^u,* Stands Erect.
54. *Mûkwû Nämesît,* Bear Stands Erect.
55. *Wapa'shi Ma'k^w,* Daylight Bear.
56. *Mûkutä'umûk^w,** Black Bear.
57. *Kwiêsähimûk^w,* Boy Bear.
58. *Mämäskwapî'nikwä°,* Red Eye Woman.
59. *Mûkwi I'nêni^u,* Small Bear Man.
60. *Mû'kasît,* Bear Foot.
61. *Mi'shîkwagâ,* Hair Above Genitals.
62. *Kiwa'si,* Climbing From Limb to Limb.
63. *Mä'sikumîgo'kwä°,* Grandmother Earth.[10]
64. *Muko'wish,* Male Bear's Head.
65. *Shê'kak,* Skunk.
66. *Wapi'kahân,* White (Bear's) Fat.

BUFFALO GENS NAMES

1. *Wä^xkûniu,* Poor Buffalo, i. e., Lean Buffalo.
2. *Nänoswi'winäo,* Buffalo Horn.
3. *Wapinî'nos,* White Buffalo.
4. *Wapinîno'sokwäo,* White Buffalo Woman.
5. *Soski'näo,* Straight Horn.

---

[10]The name Grandmother Earth occurs in the Bear Gens because Mä'siku-migo'kwäo, grandmother of Wi'sakä, had a bear paramour, according to one of the myths of the Culture Hero cycle.

6. *Wapanä'nuswa'*, All Night Buffalo.
7. *Mu'îte^u*, Dirty Behind.
8. *Mä'kasäto*, Buffalo Head or Mouth.
9. *Mami'shi^w*, Extra Tripe.
10. *Wi'sakä,** The Culture Hero.[11]
11. *Shishi'gwûn,** Gourd Rattle.[11]

WOLF GENS NAMES

1. *Meshê'^xbekwa'*, Big Ribs.
2. *Mûkatä' Muhwä^wa*, Black Wolf.
3. *Miakimi'siu*, Dung on the Road.
4. *Papamitck^xwä'sâ*, Wolf Looking Back Over His Shoulder (as he runs away).
5. *Tcûkî'muhwä^wa*, Little Wolf.
6. *Pabä'shkosît*, Mangey Wolf.
7. *Bî'gwanu*, Bushy Tail (Woman's name).
8. *Wapûnwä'tûk*, Howls Till Daylight.
9. *Mägî'simu*, Big Voice.
10. *Muhwaibû'nishâ*, Wolf Cub.[12]
11. *Äsâ'wäsi*, Bay Colored Wolf.
12. *Opi'kai'ya*, (Wolf) Rib.
13. *Ma'noshäo*, Puppies (Woman's name).
14. *Muhwä'kwä^o*, Wolf Woman.
15. *Nanomi'paho*, Trotting Wolf.
16. *Napû'mutut-Muhwä^w*, Fishing Wolf.[13]
17. *Kikiwanê'm^wo*, Stray Dog.
18. *Winî'shatûk*, Urinates on Trail.
19. *Pätê'gwishkîk*, Curls Up to Sleep.
20. *Wapi'muhwä'^wa*, White Wolf.
21. *Pokwî'muhwä^wa*, One Half a Wolf.
22. *Piä'tanokwä^o*, Wolf Den.
23. *Pokwûn Muhwä'o*, Half Wolf.
24. *Muhwä'sû',** Young Wolf.
25. *Muhwäta'*, Sounding Wolf.

---

[11]The name of the culture hero occurs in this gens because Wi'sakä raced with a buffalo, according to the myth of the origin of the Medicine Dance, and carried his rattle with him. The name Shishi'gwûn occurs likewise in the Great Sea gens, because the race was along the sea-shore.

[12]Young Wolf, Michelson.

[13]So-called because in one of the myths a wolf fished through the ice with his tail.

26. *Muhwä'sîkʷ*, Acts Like She Wolf.
27. *Ma'nwätûk*, Lots of Noise.
28. *Tanä'komiᵘ*, Walks Through Deep Water (Mythological reference).
29. *Mûkutä Ä'sipûn*, Black Raccoon.
30. *Wab Ä'sipun,** White Raccoon (This name is used by the Menomini for dogs when eaten ceremonially).
31. *Ya'patä,** From the Wolf Brother of Wi'sakä, who was slain by the Underworld Panthers. Said to mean "Lies in the Sun to Bask."
32. *Muhwä'sa,** Wolf-like. This is the alternate name for Ya'patä among the Menomini.
33. *Mûkutä'wänîm*, Black Dog.

TURKEY GENS NAMES

1. *Penä'kwä°*, Turkey Hen (Woman's name).
2. *Nishkê'ˣkât*, Gobbles Strutting.
3. *Kwi'êsä*, Boy, i. e., young male turkey.
4. *Skwäˣsä*, Girl, i. e., young turkey hen.
5. *Na'pîtut*, Turkey Beard.
6. *Wi'shkwînäwâ*, Gobbler.
7. *Apê'mêkinabâ*, Roosting Above.
8. *Wápûna'piᵘ*, Stands (on tree) Till Dawn.
9. *Mä'skokâ*, Red Wattles.
10. *Katûkâ'kä*, Spotted Wings.
11. *Wapagu'näskûk*, White Tracks on Snow.
12. *Näkwaski'paho*, Hiding in Weeds.
13. *Tci'känä°*, Comb of Turkey.
14. *Nä'kwakiᵘ*, Hides His Head.
15. *Wapi'pênäo*, White Turkey.
16. *Wayä'pênäo*, Turkey Beard.
17. *Nä'muskwipäho*, Erect Runner.
18. *Kêtci'paka'kwa*, Big Cock.
19. *Kêno'äbâ*, Roosting Sideways.
20. *Pokwî'nêkwat*, Crippled Turkey.
21. *Pämiki'witä*, Stays in Timbered Bottoms.
22. *Shigwamiᵘ*, Leaving the Nest.
23. *Witâ'gâ*, Wings on Both Sides.

FISH GENS NAMES

1. *Mûtci' Nêmäs,* Bad Fish.
2. *Wapi'nêmäo,* White Sturgeon.
3. *Ki'shamäkʷ,* Already Fish.
4. *Nêmäo,** Sturgeon.
5. *Känwî'känäo,* Pointed Head, i. e., Sturgeon.
6. *Keo'kûk,* Circling.
7. *Kwa'skami,* Scattering Out.
8. *Mokoho'ko,* Showing Himself.
9. *Päshi'pähu,* Fish Rubbing Bank.
10. *Wisupiagê'tu,* Fish Breaking Water. Also used as a teasing form of ceremonial address by a man to his nephew, if the latter happens to be of the Fish gens, and especially on public occasions.
11. *Ta'ˣkinikʷ,* Cold Eyes.
12. *Wa'pamäkʷ,* White Catfish.
13. *Wi'shokʷ,* Yellow Catfish.
14. *Wa'sêsiû,* Bullhead.
15. *Mûkätämia'nämäkʷ,* Black Forktail Catfish.
16. *Mûtcikwäwa,* Ugly Faced Fish.
17. *Wi'kêtcä,* Buffalo Fish.
18. *Nämä'sikwäº,* Fish Woman.
19. *Sho'skwonêtʷ,* Slips Out of the Hand.
20. *Sho'skohut,* Glances (from spear).
21. *Kû'nwaska,* Frog.
22. *Namäpiäkitûna'wätûk,* Shouts Under Water.
23. *Wûha'gîsäº,* Exposing Head.
24. *Miy'anomäʷ,* Not Eating Fish Clean.
25. *Wä'wakiᵘ,* Swimming Crookedly.
26. *A'shika,* Young Bass.
27. *A'sikan,* Bass.
28. *Si'kûmäkʷ,* Gar.
29. *Skutäo,* Fire (because fire was used to fish with at night and also to cook fish with).
30. *Mûkûte Si'kûmäkʷ,* Black Gar.
31. *Mûkûte A'sikûn,* Black Bass.
32. *Wi'sûkûtäº,** Sunfish.
33. *Kêtûk Kûmaho,* Spotted Sunfish.
34. *Wi'kätcä,* Buffalo Fish.
35. *Pä'shito,* Old Man (Name of Drumfish).

36. *Wapama'k*, White (cat) Fish.
37. *Mê'shinomäk*, Giant Fish (Mythological).
38. *Wapi' Nämä°*, White Sturgeon.
39. *Okäwûk*, Pike (plural).
40. *Maskwa'sêkwahûk*, Suckers.
41. *Pu*ᵡ*kê'tuhûk*, Chubs.
42. *Wäwikä*, House Owner (reference to a fish nest).

GREAT SEA GENS NAMES

1. *Kê'tcikûmi*, Great Sea.
2. *Wase'djuam*, Bright Flowing Water.
3. *Mäshîsi'pu*, Mississippi, or "Great River."
4. *Tcûkisi'pu*, Little River.
5. *Mûtcisi'pu,** Bad River.
6. *Pêshi'wa*, Wild Cat, i. e., one of the Underneath Panthers of Mythology.
7. *Manêtu'kä°*, Mermaid, literally God, or Snake Woman.
8. *Pemi'tûnu*, Passing Water.
9. *Kiwatû'nu*, Eddying Backwards.
10. *Wawia'tûnu*, Whirlpool.
11. *Kishkitû'nukä°*, Waterfall.
12. *Kwaskwitû'ng'*, Riffles.
13. *Kêtcikûmi'kwä°*, Great Sea Woman.
14. *Piwä'kumi*ᵘ, Back Flowing Ocean.
15. *Witê'ko*ᵃ, Waves, i. e., Surf.
16. *Paia'si*ᵘ, Bubbles (under the ice).
17. *Mêsîk*, Ice.
18. *Têtêpitûng',** Eddy.
19. *Utê'ku*ᵃ,** Wave.
20. *Witê'kokwä°*, Surf Woman.
21. *Askipûki'kûmi*, Green Bay (named from the old Sauk home on Green Bay, Wisconsin).
22. *Askipûkikû'mikwä°*, Green Bay Woman.
23. *Tishu'kûmi*, Warm Sea.
24. *Wa'pikûmi*, White Sea.
25. *Wisko'säo*, Lake Wisconsin, i. e., Lake Michigan.
26. *Mû'tcinêp*ⁱ, Bad Water.
27. *Wasi'kûmikwä°*, Moonlight on the Sea Woman.
28. *Meshikwatätä'pâhokwût*, Ice Cake Floating on the Ocean.

29. *Kä^xkîtûnuk^w*, Mark on the Water Woman.
30. *Kämiâ,* Rain.
31. *Kêtcisha'wan,* Great Sprinkling (on the surface of the sea).
32. *Hähäo,* Swan (also Thunder gens name. Included here because its habitat is on the sea).
33. *Mänitu'wä,* Water Spirit or Serpent.¹⁴
34. *Na'mpêshik^w,* Underworld Panther Woman.¹⁴
35. *Pêshik^w,* Lynx Woman.¹⁴
36. *Mê'shikä°,* Snapping Turtle.¹⁴
37. *Shi'shigwûn,* Gourd, i. e., Rattle.¹⁴

THUNDER GENS NAMES

1. *Sawîn Inêmäkiu,* Yellow Thunder.
2. *Wapîn Inê'mäkiu,* White Thunder.
3. *Mêsikwa'kä,* Ice on Wings.
4. *Mû'kute Mi'shikäkäk,* Black Hawk.
5. *Wasêho'nokwä°,* Light in Front, i. e., of the Thunderers.
6. *Kwago'hosi^u,* Sounding Ahead.
7. *Skutä'o,* Fire.
8. *Tca'kênä°,* (Thunder-bird), "Eating Serpent."
9. *Konêpakä,* Soaring.
10. *Piä'tcîsût^w,* Flying Over.
11. *Piä'tcisä^{kw},* Flying over Woman.
12. *Piätana'^xkahûk,* Strikes Top Branches.
13. *Bäkûtûk,* Tree Striker.
14. *Nika'nûkohûk,* Leader in Striking.
15. *Wamê'soni^u,* All Body, i. e., reference to one of the snakes eaten by Thunder Birds.
16. *Nê'nêmäkis^a,* Little Thunder.
17. *Pi'ätwätûk,* Coming Noise.
18. *Nä'kutwätûk,* One Noise.
19. *Nûwakwä'geshûk,* Middle of the Day.
20. *Sawa'nakwût,* Yellow Cloud.
21. *Mûkû'täwâkwût,* Black Cloud.
22. *Notê'n,* Wind.

---

¹⁴This group of names is included in the Ocean gens because the Underworld Horned Panther, a mythical long-tailed, horned monster dwells in seas, lakes, rivers, etc., under water. The lynx or wildcat is its representative on earth. The Snapping Turtle and the Merman and Mermaid are of course included because of their habitat. The Gourd is an Ocean gens name, because in one of the myths Snapping Turtle carries a gourd rattle in a race.

23. *Notê'no'käo*, Coming Winds.
24. *Mûkutê Ninîmäki^u*, Black Thunder.
25. *Mûtci-kîneu,** Bad (in the sense of terrible) Eagle.
26. *Pi'äjisât*, Flying Over.
27. *Piäta'nokwi^u*, Coming Storm.
28. *Mêskwä'makwi^u*, Red Cloud in Storm.
29. *Aia'tci^u*, Starts (thundering) Afresh.
30. *Kishkanaka'hak,** Tree Breaker.
31. *Wapa'bkwokûk*, White Streak (On Stricken Tree).
32. *Tä'pasi^u*, Circling Above.
33. *Wapiki'shko*, White Ki'shko.[15]
34. *Ki'shko*, Ki'shko.[15]
35. *Oskû'sh*, Oskû'sh.[15]
36. *Nu^xkagê*, Tender Wings.
37. *Mê'shikä*, Snapping Turtle.
38. *Tukû'misä^o,** Flying Across the Trail.
39. *Wapimi'kwûn*, White Feather.
40. *Kwäkwäjîsä*, Learning to Fly.
41. *Pa^xkêtu*, Distant Flash.
42. *Wapi'jikwä*, White Face.
43. *Tcakäta'gosi^u*, Heard All Over.
44. *Wase^xhono^xkwê*, Light After Storm.
45. *Täka'koskûk*, Passing Shadow.
46. *Mämäkä*, Butterfly.
47. *Notê'nokwä^o*, Wind Woman.
48. *Pemiwa'käk^w*, Moulting Feather (Woman's name).

BEAR-POTATO GENS NAMES

1. *Nika'piä*, Vining Out.
2. *Katûwhan*, Digging Potatoes.
3. *Anänotäo Pä'niäk*, Known by Indians as Potatoes.
4. *Ki'shkänâ*, Breaking the Vine.
5. *Kä'ta^xhank*, Being Dug Out.
6. *Kätûhoku^x*, Washed Out by High Water.
7. *Pä'niak Sa'giwûk*, Potato Sprouts.
8. *Wapo'so*, Stains the Water.

---

[15]The Thunderers, like the Sauk themselves, are supposed to be divided into two moieties, Ki'shko, painting in white, and Oskû'sh painting in black. The Oskû'sh division as among the Sauk goes ahead and does not turn back. The Oskû'sh make all the fuss and noise. While both are enemies of the Horned Serpents, it is the Oskû'sh who do the killing, and the Ki'shko eat the victims.

9. *Sake'je*siu*, Exposed Potato Root.
10. *Kiwapiyû*, Potato Vine.
11. *Sasaki'huk*, Bunches of Tubers Together.
12. *Mê'skutc*, Reddish (color).
13. *Kiwa'pishi^u*, In the Way, i. e., the Potato Vine.
14. *Koskima'hûk*, Potato Vine Seeds.

BEAVER GENS NAMES

1. *Kiskikû'tcikä^o*, Biter Off of Roots.
2. *O'mäk^w*, Beaver.
3. *Gapi^{x}kän'uk*, Beaver Dam.
4. *Täpopo'siu*, Level Full of Water.
5. *Kätîkänuk^w*, Damming the Creek.
6. *Wagî'kanuk^w*, Crooked Dam.
7. *Kiwîkanuk^w*, Dams the Branches.
8. *Pena'tci^u*, Tears Holes in the Dam.
9. *Tcû'komä'k^w*, Little Beaver.
10. *I'womäk^w*, Known as a Beaver.
11. *Kiwî'tcîmä^w*, Swing Around, i. e., action of beaver in swimming.
12. *Piätci'tcimä^w*, Swing Round Towards Me.
13. *Kakî'suta^x*, Hiding in Den.
14. *Wa'bomêk^w*, White Beaver.
15. *'Ki'omêk^w*, Small Beaver.
16. *Tcûkiomêk^w*, Little Beaver.
17. *Wawanikâ'hîtcimä^w*, Cuts Willow with His Teeth.
18. *Gäwûtcikä^w*, Gnaws Down Trees.

EAGLE GENS NAMES

1. *Mê^{x}gêsiu*, Bald Eagle.
2. *Wa'pikêti^{wa}*, White Eagle.
3. *Mudji'kêti^w*,* Bad or Ugly Eagle.
4. *Kê'ti^{wa}*, Eagle.
5. *Keti'sa^x*, Eaglet.
6. *Mû'kûte Kêti^w*, Black Eagle.
7. *Tcûki' Kêti^w*, Little Eagle.
8. *Mê^{x}gêsiu O'kima*, Bald Eagle Chief.
9. *Wapêskîtäpä*, White Headed Eagle.

10. *Kêti^xkwe^w*, Eagle Woman.
11. *Mêkêsi'ta*, Erect Sitting Eagle.
12. *Wapi'kakê*, White Breast.
13. *Name'akwîsâ,** Swift Flying.
14. *Pä'misiwa*, Greasy Feather.
15. *Mûkûtemîshikä'käk*, Black Duck Hawk.
16. *Witê^xkoa*, Owl.
17. *Muskute Witê^xkoa*, Prairie Owl.
18. *Ti'tiwa*, Blue Jay.
19. *Pishki'nani^u*, Locust.
20. *Pitaski^w*, Dragon Fly.

FOX GENS NAMES[16]

1. *Wa'kushä,** Fox.
2. *Tcû'kiwakushä*, Little Fox.
3. *Nana'hiki^u*, Young Growing Fox.
4. *Wagasha'siu*, Foxlike.
5. *Pikwa'noⁿ*, Bushy Tail.
6. *Tca'kikwat*, Small Face.
7. *Sho'skêsh*, Straight Ears.
8. *Sha'kwäni^u*, Deepset Eyes.
9. *Wi'shkosä°*, Raised Off the Ground (in running).
10. *Sho'kwi^{wa}*, Soft Walking.
11. *Kû'pahi^x*, Sly Mover.
12. *Wätcinä'witcî*, Why He Sees Me.
13. *Sa'waⁿik^w*, Fox Squirrel.
14. *Kê'shkashe O'kema*, Peaceable Chief.

DEER GENS NAMES

1. *Wapiska'nûwä°*, White Tail.
2. *Sisia'*, White Tail. (Another form of No. 1.)
3. *Wasiinä'osä°*, Bright Horn.
4. *Sagikiwinä'kapâ*, Horns Sticking Out.
5. *Mäkûte Wi'kwägâ*, Black Necked Buck.
6. *Kêtca'iapäo*, Big Buck.
7. *Oko'^a*, Doe.
8. *Pêshî'gîshikwä°*, Deer Woman.

---

[16]Fox Gens names are very like those of the Wolf Gens, and some are said to be interchangeable.

9. *Mako'sikwä°*, Doe Fawn.[17]
10. *Shoski'winäo*, Straight Horn.
11. *Mishîwînât*, Velvet Horns.
12. *Mishiga'kwa*, Yearling Buck.
13. *Kätûkänä°*, Spotted Fawn.
14. *Wapa°sai°*, White Tanned Deer Hide.
15. *Kê'tcimä*, Old Elk.
16. *Ma°kini°*, Elk Fawn.
17. *Wawa'tusä*, Deer Meeting.
18. *Tänwa'piäshîk*, Lying Down Stretched Out.
19. *A'iyapäo*, Buck.
20. *Oshä'ki°*, Ridge (Deer run along ridges).
21. *Mätêkomi'näkäo*, Hunts Small Acorns.
22. *Päguwi'käwä*, Makes Dust on Trail.
23. *Tu'kigûsh*, Spreading Hoofs.
24. *Namia'shîkgo*, Bad Nose (of deer).
25. *Wasi'shîmuk*, Partly Visible.
26. *Nänyä'skwi°*, Weaned Fawn.
27. *Oka'kaia*, Brisket.
28. *Notê'nwikwä°*, Runs Up Wind.
29. *Mä'shkoikwä°*, Bloody Face (from buck's fighting).
30. *Wapi'kwat*, White Face or Eyes.
31. *Mûtci Mukêsä*, Bad Moccasin.
32. *Wapê'shkêsi°*, White Deer Woman.
33. *Wapai'apäo*, White Buck.
34. *Mäsâwênât*, Two Spike Buck.

MARRIAGE CUSTOMS

Among the Sauk marriages were generally arranged by the parents of the contracting parties. The parents of a girl, for example, would select an eligible young man and then interview his father and mother. If all was agreeable sometimes the marriage was consummated the next day. The parents of the bride would get up a feast and take it straightway over to the groom's lodge. The young man's parents would dress the girl in fine clothes and give her a horse and plenty of household utensils. The youth then went to live with the girl in her parent's home.

[17]From the Myth of Wisaka and Turtle. To be published in a later bulletin.

The punishment meted out to a woman for adultery was to have her hair or nose cropped, usually the penalty was inflicted by her own brothers. For minor offenses the woman's uncles might beat her.

If a woman was widowed, and was held in high esteem by the parents of her husband, after she had fasted part of each day and mourned for thirty days, they would dress her in good clothes and marry her to one of her husband's brothers or some other male relative.

When a man's wife died, her relatives took everything in the home, regardless of whether it was his or hers, leaving only a saddle, gun, and blanket, and helping themselves not only to such valuable property as horses, but even to sweet corn and other food. In the case of the death of the wife of a man who was an accredited Brave, or Watâ'säº, he was left alone, and nothing was disturbed.

A widower fasted part of each day for from thirty to forty days, after which his relatives brought him new clothes and goods to make up for those taken from him. His brothers-in-law then shaved his head, painted his face, and sent him out to find a new mate.

A man may not speak to his mother-in-law, nor a woman to her father-in-law. Joking may be indulged in with one's brothers and sisters-in-law, and one's uncles and aunts.

Plurality of wives was formerly in vogue.

Just as among the Menomini, where "Manabus's blanket" is said to have been used formerly to prevent physical contact between married couples, the Sauk had a similar custom. The robe, of deerskin, was called Pwaˣhigûn or Maˣkunan, and was kept by certain persons and loaned or hired out especially to newly married couples so that their skins would not touch during connection. It was adorned with jinglers so that all might know when and how intercourse was being held. The reason assigned for this custom was in order that "no children born to members of the tribe might be strange or deformed."

TRAINING OF CHILDREN

WINTER FASTING

During the winter boys were given one meal a day. The youngest ones, however, only went without breakfast. They were also not allowed to drink. This fasting was kept up from the fall until the frogs began to sing in the spring.

Certain old men in camp used to lecture and harangue the boys daily. Our informant states that he has seen as many as possible of the boys of a village assembled in a bark house listening to an old man hold forth, while others were crowded around the outside, sitting on the ground and remaining there for hours.

At the beginning of the winter fasting season the adult men of the tribe would seek out small basswood saplings standing alone, and cut them down, making them into ten-inch peeled lengths. The ends of these were charred for blackening the faces of fasters, and two of them would last a man all winter. They were called Mûkûte wi'tcikûn, or "Black (Fasting) Sticks," and were hung up in the lodge among the sacred articles. They were carefully put away when the first frogs' songs were heard. This custom is also found among the Ioway.

It is said that the two tribal moieties, Ki'shko and Oskû'sh used to vie with each other to see who could first use up an equal number of sticks of a given length.

DREAM FASTING

When at or about the age of puberty, about fourteen years, both boys and girls were formerly required to fast and thus incubate a dream in which some supernatural power appeared to the supplicant and volunteered itself as a Dream Guardian. Fasters blackened their faces and repaired to some isolated spot where they gazed at the rising sun, so that it, their "Grandfather," would recognize them thereafter as persons who had fasted.

The powers of whom the Sauk children tried to dream were Shawanû'täsiu; the South God or Wind, who appeared generally as a monster serpent; the God of the Sea, or Kêtcikûmi manitu; the Thunder, who always gave success in war, and the Buffalo or Bear, either of which gave good hunting medicine. Of course, other powers often appeared, but these were the ones most desired.

FIRST GAME FEAST

When a child kills his first game, no matter how small and insignificant it may be, a ceremony called Kikikä'nu[a] or feast of the first game is held. The little creature is cooked in a kettle, with other food, and the neighbors are called in. The animal killed by the little boy is placed in a special wooden bowl and set before his uncle, who eats it all, with great show of ceremony and profuse thanks to encourage the youthful nimrod. This is a widespread Algonkian custom.

RELIGION

CONCEPTIONS OF DEITIES

Gêtci Mû′nito^a is though to be an old white-headed man of majestic appearance who sits everlastingly in the Heavens, smoking. While it has been the fashion in recent years for many writers to maintain that the Great Spirit concept is wholly of missionary origin among the Indians, Father Claude Allouez, the first missionary to visit the Sauk, declares that they, with the Fox and Potawatomi, were already in possession of this belief. In the Jesuit Relation for the years 1666-1667 he states, speaking of the Fox: "These people are not very far removed from the recognition of the Creator of the world, for it is they who told me what I have already related,—namely, that they acknowledge in their country a great spirit, the maker of Heaven and earth, who dwells in the country toward the French."

Whatever may ultimately be shown to be the case among the tribes of other areas, there can be no doubt as to the antiquity of the Great Spirit among the Central Algonkians, and perhaps elsewhere in the woodlands, although it is likely that many of these peoples formerly looked upon the sun as this supreme deity.

Wi′sakä, the culture hero, founder of the Medicine Dance, dwells on earth in the north. He is of human appearance, and will some day return to deliver his uncles and aunts, the Indians, from the white man's yoke. A similar belief is found among the Menomini.

The Thunderers, called Nê′nêmîkiwûk or Wä′migohûk, the latter term being a ceremonial form of address meaning "The Feathered Ones," are generally considered, as by most woodland Indians, to be giant eagles inhabiting the western Empyrean, but some maintain that they resemble human beings, or, at least, are anthropomorphic at times. They dress like men, and wear especially elegant fringed leather leggings.

The Water Spirits consist of monstrous snakes and enormous panthers who dwell everywhere in waterfalls and dismal swamps, springs, etc. The serpents are constantly preyed upon by the Thunderbirds, who eat them, but sometimes the serpents have revenge.   It is said that some of them hold a Thunderer captive beneath Niagara Falls, and that when he hears his brethren during a storm he cries to them, and lightnings may be seen flashing in the east (reflections) whenever there is a storm in the west. With all their power, however, the Thunderbirds cannot free him, for the mighty rock ledge over which the cataract falls is impervious to their bolts.

Four of the great serpents support "this island," the earth, on their backs. Their leader is called Kwägwä'shiwäo, and he was once killed by Wi'sakä, but lives again, as he is immortal.

The giant Underworld Panthers, Nampe'ˣshiwûk, have spotted bodies like wildcats, and tails of immense length. They, and the Thunderers also, often appear in conventionalized designs on woven bags, and, more rarely, on mats.

Tepä'kininiʷᵃ, the "night man," who frightens belated travelers, is known as a spirit or power on earth. Under the name of Tepä'inäniᵘ, he is known to the Menomini.

Skutä'näsiu is the "Master of Fire," a God connected with the underworld serpents.

The Ukima manêtu'wûk, "Chief Snakes or Powers," are regarded as benevolent, because they do not bite. They are represented on earth by the "bull snakes."

Kêtcikûmi Manitu is the God of the Sea, while the Paia'shiwûk are two brothers, dwarfs, who dwell under the water.

Mä'sakomigo'kwäᵒ, "Our Grandmother, the Earth," is the earth personified as an old woman. She figures prominently in Sauk mythology as the old grandmother who raised the hero Wi'sakä. She is frequently invoked and to her are offered tobacco sacrifices which are buried in the ground. She owns the roots and herbs which are the hairs of her head. Under a similar name she figures in Menomini mythology.

Shawa'natäsiu is the manitu of the south. Just what his properties and functions are, besides controlling the warm winds, are not apparent. He is personified as a great serpent, and was desired as a dream guardian.

Ya'patä is the brother of Wi'sakä, the Culture Hero, and has charge of the realm of the Dead. As Ona'ˣpatäo, this personage is known to the Menomini.

Po'kîtäpäwä, known as "Knocks-a-hole-in-the-head" or "Brain

Taker," guards the bridge on the trail to the afterworld. He attempts to dash out the brains of all passing souls, who must escape him to win their way to the other world. A somewhat similar notion is found among the Menomini, where the souls are robbed of a pinch of their brains by "Na'ˣpatäo the ruler himself, before they enter the Land of the Dead.

It is quite probable that there are a number of other deities, spirits, monsters, and hobgoblins known to the Sauk, whose names and characteristics still remain unrecorded.

THE HEREAFTER

No person is possessed of more than one soul, and this leaves the body at once for the Afterworld as soon as a person dies. It follows the Milky Way (Wabise'pu, the White River), until it arrives at the river which all Sauk must cross before entering the Afterworld, which is controlled by Ya'patä, brother of Wi'sakä. A log serves for a bridge, and this is guarded by a being called Po'kîtäpäwä, "Knocks-a-hole-in-the-head," or "Brain Taker." Brain Taker has a watch dog who barks the alarm whenever a new soul approaches, and the fleeting spirit must be swift indeed to avoid having his brains dashed out. If this happens, he is destroyed or lost forever, but if he eludes Brain Taker he darts across the log to the abode of the dead, where there is everlasting feasting and rejoicing.

MORTUARY CUSTOMS

When a person dies, the mourners blacken their faces, dishevel their hair, and fast, eating only at night, and, rising early in the morning they face the east and wail. This is continued for from four to ten days, although the late Mêshê'bêkwa is said to have once mourned in this manner for forty days.

If the deceased is a chief or belongs to a chief's family, his face is painted green (equivalent of blue, the holy sky color) at once. Wm. Harris, as a member of a chief's family, was once called upon to paint the remains of a woman of equally high lineage. With green paint he made an oblong square across her breast, and another across her forehead, reaching from ear to ear. An ordinary man is always painted by his uncles, a woman by her aunts. No clan or moiety customs were found in connection with the dead.

The night following the death, a feast is held, and next morning the corpse is dressed for the grave. The body is then placed in a blanket and carried out, usually through the side or back of the wigwam or through a window if in the house. No reason for this could be gathered, but, judging by the cognate belief of the more conservative Menomini, this is done to confuse the spirit of the dead person so that it will not be able to come back and haunt the survivors. Among the Sauk the hopelessly sick are taken outside to die. If a person dies indoors, the house is abandoned and later burned.

The body is carried to the grave, feet forward, the blanket being knotted at the ends and slung over a pole supported by several men. The grave, narrow and shallow, is excavated by women, who use wooden bowls as spades. The body is lowered into the grave, and tobacco is thrown upon it. An old man is now elected to address the corpse and tell it how to reach the other world. After he has finished, all those present approach the grave and sprinkle tobacco on the corpse. Those who carry him to the grave are usually of the moiety, Oskû'sh or Kî'shko, to which the deceased belonged.

After the ceremony, the widow, in returning home, makes a wide circle from west to east. Next day all the mourners rise especially early to wail.

In burying the dead, the people of the Turkey Clan have certain peculiar customs. Their fellow gens members are always buried sitting upright, as a turkey sleeps. They are not buried in a general cemetery, but on some isolated knoll under a tree suitable for a turkey roost.

The Handbook of American Indians states that among the Sauk both tree and scaffold burial were practiced, also complete burial in the earth, and surface burial in a sitting posture in several forms. These may have been styles in vogue in different gentes, but inquiry shows that these are now forgotten.

NOTES ON THE MEDICINE DANCE

The following data were secured from the Reverend Wm. Harris, who stated that he had never been made a member of the Medicine Lodge, but that he had for many years been one of the native police who were charged with maintaining order at the public performances, preventing the near approach of spectators, and the like. He had heard the recitation of the rituals, was familiar with the rites, and knew some of the songs. The data here presented are therefore no doubt entirely correct, so far as they go, but lack the detail which can only be obtained from a master of the craft. Owing to the complete mystery with which the Sauk rites are enshrouded, and the need of further light on the ceremony from this important tribe, no apology is made for publishing this incomplete fragment.

THE ORIGIN MYTH

The world had already existed for some time when Wi'sakä was born, and the hero lived alone with his brother Ya'patäo and their grandmother Mäsûkûmigo'kwäo, the Earth Woman.

Wi'sakä roamed about over the earth's surface and slew many great serpents, until at length the survivors all convened in a council. To this meeting they invited the grandmother of Wi'sakä.

"Grandmother," said the Underworld Serpents, "Your eldest grandson is abusing us so that we want to destroy him in some way."

"It is useless to try it," answered the old woman, "Wi'sakä is immortal. Yet maybe you have power to kill his younger brother." So, in revenge, the Serpents planned to end Wi'sakä's younger brother, Ya'patäo, in the following way: They challenged Wi'sakä to race with a three-year-old buffalo. The course was to encircle Kêtcikûm (Lake Michigan). As soon as the contestants had rounded the opposite shore, the Serpents attacked Ya'patäo. Even where he was, Wi'sakä could hear his younger brother crying for assistance. It seemed to him as though Ya'patäo had called, "Oh, my elder brother, they are killing me!"

Then Wi'sakä ran all the faster, and as he drew towards home, he passed the buffalo. Still he ran faster, and as he got nearer home he could hear his younger brother plainly calling: "Oh, my elder brother Wi'sakä, they are killing me!" But when Wi'sakä arrived at the place, it was too late. They had already killed his younger brother Ya'patäo, and skinned him and carried the skin away.

Then Wi'sakä went into mourning. He blackened his face, then he attacked and killed the Underworld monsters with redoubled fury, until the Great Serpents relented and feared him. At last they appealed to Gêtci Mû'nito[a], the Great Spirit. They counciled with him and at his advice decided to build a Medicine Lodge Structure, a Mitä'wigan. Then they sent a hawk to call Wi'sakä.

Three times the hawk carried the invitation to Wi'sakä, but he was lying there weeping, with his face blackened, and did not look up. When the hawk appeared for the fourth time, Wi'sakä raised his head, "What do they want me for?" he asked.

"Gêtci Mû'nito^a sends for you," replied the hawk.

When Wi'sakä heard that the Great Spirit himself had sent for him, his heart dropped down, and he became less angry than he was formerly. So he arose and followed the hawk. But when he arrived at the Mitä'wigan, he saw that they had stretched his brother's hide and were using it for a door, and again his heart rose into his mouth and almost choked him. Yet, when the door was opened for him, Wi'sakä went in.

The lodge was long and low, it was placed so that the ends, in which there were doors, were faced east and west. In the northeast corner sat Gêtci Mû'nito^a, and Wi'sakä was given a seat on his right, with his back against a burr oak pole. Gêtci Mû'nito^a led the ceremonies himself, and when he saw this, all Wi'sakä's anger left him.

Now all the Munêtu'wuk, or Spirits, were called into the Lodge— that is, all except the Thunderers, who were not invited. Otherwise all the Spirits were there, including the black bear and the grizzly bear. Then they instructed Wi'sakä and appointed a time, four days later, for him to return for initiation.

Then Wi'sakä went home to his grandmother, Mäsûkûmigo'kwäo, the Earth Woman. He lay down to rest, but no sooner had he done so than his younger brother, Ya'patäo, approached his wigwam, crying:

"Here am I, my elder brother! Let me in!"

"No," responded Wi'sakä, "I cannot admit you!"

Again Ya'patäo begged him. "Let me in, my elder brother!"

"No," answered Wi'sakä, "I cannot admit you."

Still his younger brother besought him. "Admit me, elder brother." And still Wi'sakä refused him entrance.

Then for the fourth time Ya'patäo pleaded, "Let me in, oh elder brother!"

This time Wi'sakä responded: "It cannot be, my younger brother, I must not let you in—but here is a little drum and here is a sacred whistle. Go west through the Heavens to the other world where the Dancing Ground (of the dead) is located. Every time you beat your drum our uncles and aunts will come to you" (i. e., new persons will die).

Then Ya'patäo took the whistle and blew upon it, and struck his drum. Lo, at once there were five or six souls of newly dead persons standing beside him. These accompanied him on his journey to the other world, where he remains forever as chief. At the end of four days' time, the lodge was ready and Wi'sakä went there, where the Manitous were gathered. There were present all kinds of serpents and beasts who had been invited to the Mitä'in. The drum was placed in the northeast corner of the structure, where Gêtci Mû'nito^a was, and he commenced the ceremony. The guests were seated beside him beginning with Wi'sakä on his right and running in order towards the left. That is the order which we follow today, and, in the initiation the candidate, male or female, impersonates Wi'sakä and takes part in the re-enactment of the ceremony of his initiation.

THE CEREMONY OF INITIATION

The lodge is placed so that the doors in its ends face east and west, and the candidate is seated in the northeast corner beside the Master of Ceremonies, to whom he has applied for admission. His back is to a burr oak stake, and the drum is in the same corner before the Master of Ceremonies. The others present range around the lodge beginning on the candidate's right, going to the left. The sacred drum circulates in this order, each person using it to accompany four songs, and when it gets back to its starting point, the first part is over and the feast commences. A gourd rattle is also used, which is struck against a pillow carried on the left arm.

When the members enter the Medicine Lodge structure, they sing a song known as the "Entering Song," which is, of course, four times repeated. It is:

Nipa'nina-a-a kiwise' woho asowakumike hojisewo nepanina'.

"My arrow (the migis shell) is flying round, it even came from the other world."

As they chant this song the members hold their "otter skins" out before them at the level of their shoulders, and shake the heads of the animals. While this is going on the younger members from several bands, led in each case by an older man, go to the west end of the lodge and face the east where they all stand and sing the same song again. Then they circle the lodge, holding their "otter skins" out in front of them, making them move as though swimming, and crying "Tcû ihihi'," without limit. On the fourth round they circle the fire and return to their starting point, where all the younger members shoot themselves and fall over. When the leader of each group is shot, he falls over the drum and lies while this song is sung:

Ho' kutakami, kutakami, tci'paipa kutakami.

"Dead man's lungs."

This is kept up four times, when the leader revives. The leader then takes charge once more. He sings:

Yuhähä'hä, Yuhähä'hä, mûnipapiyuni kätayutänänä.

"This real medicine, I am using it on you."

Another shooting song is as follows:

Hamwa'kani, hamwa'kani hanimohä nakwita, hamwa'kani, hamwa'-kani, Watâsä' hamwa'kani!

"Eating, eating, a fat dog, eating. A brave man to eat, eating."

When this performance is over the two leaders go to the east end of the structure and sing while the rest sit still. The drum has been left in the center of the lodge, but one of the leaders carries the rattle and pillow. He motions with his gourd to all to bow their heads. The song is:

Wapikonä woho', wapikonä woho', nakapäkwä piwatci, yohaniyä, wi hi hi hi hi!

"That place, that place, where you are going to stay."

When this has been repeated four times, the leader and his assistant go to the other end of the lodge and repeat the song. After this they take up the drum and circle the lodge, the drummer in the rear, drumming, while both cry "Djû' hi hi hi hi!" This likewise is done four times. They then take the drum to the next band leader and whisper to him that he must be quick so that they can all be through by eating time.

When this is over, the waiters are sent out to fetch in the pots of food, which they sling on a pole between them. This food they give to other groups than their own. No salt or condiments are permitted. Each brave who has served as a guard gets a kettle containing a whole boiled dog to eat with his own friends. By the way, neither braves or waiters are necessarily members of the lodge. Our informant, as a member of the Bear gens and an experienced waiter, served in that capacity at Medicine Dances for years, yet was not a member.

The principal ingredients of the feast are a dog or dogs, singed, cut up, and boiled; pumpkins, and sweet corn. If the giver of any part

of the feast wishes to invite a friend among the members to eat with
him and his party, he must circle the lodge to the right until he comes
to him, even though that person may be close to him on the left. The
servants who bring in and take out the food must do the same, circling
the fire with the utensils on entering and leaving.

After the feast the drum again starts with the leader in the northeast corner, and makes its regular circuit as before. With this difference: now the singing must be faster, for now the candidate must be
initiated before the drum gets back to its starting point, where it is
carried across the eastern doorway.

Directly after the feast, the following songs are sung:

Henêni muhwä'ʷᵃ onäpi kaio'ni nanotakwatoni.

"The male wolf's ribs are howling."

Mûkûtä muhwä'ʷᵃ hênäpi kaio'ni nanotakwatoni.

"Black wolf's ribs are howling."

The order of the next performance is as follows: Several songs
occurring in sets of four are sung, the younger members rising and
dancing before the leaders, who, with the older members stand and
point the heads of their "otters" toward the singers. After the dance,
all circle back and sit down. The musicians then announce that they
will sing dancing and shooting songs, and beg all present to overlook
any mistakes should they be made. They sing a short song which is:

Winapima, winapimi.

Of this, no translation, if indeed there is any, was secured. The new
member is cautioned to shoot only his uncles, aunts, brothers and
sisters-in-law. At this time they also sing:

Säsakwitähä'.

"Bad heart" or "Crushed heart."

The words of this song refer to the feeling of the candidate as he
is shot, when it is said "he feels as though he were about to vomit."

While these things are going on, some of the older men among
the members hold up their medicine otters above their heads shouting,
"Woha! Woha!" and daring the others to shoot them. The candidate's
face is now painted, and this song is sung:

Hanamona keminanaha.

"I am giving you red paint."

Waiters spread a new blanket on the floor at the eastern end of the
building, under the ridge pole from which are suspended the can-

didate's blankets, calicoes, and other fees of admission. The candidate, attended by a monitor, is placed on the blanket, facing west.

Now two old Masters of the Craft circle the lodge, otterskin medicine bags in their hands, bending over, singing, and pretending, dramatically, to track the candidate down. At the west end they halt. They face the candidate, and make a speech, telling what they are about to do. Then they hold their "otters" outstretched before them, with their heads toward the candidate, and shake them in a serpentine manner as though they (the otters) were swimming. As they do this, they utter the medicine cry.

In this manner they sing four songs, after which they turn and point their bags east, south, west and north, crying "Hohohoho!" as they do so, and singing four sacred songs to each point of the compass.

The leader now remains standing, and makes a speech, telling the members what his powers are, of his sacred dream, and dream guardian, and promises to use all his powers to strengthen the candidate and give him long life. As he does this, his assistant goes to the western door and seats himself.

The leader now circles the lodge with his otter skin held before him, crying "Yihihihihi," until he gets in front of the candidate, where he stops and addresses him. Attendants now approach the neophyte, and stand by to place him in readiness to be shot.

The chief initiator, who is facing the candidate, now suddenly jerks the head of the otter bag upward, pointing it into his own face, and "shooting" himself. The term implies that the essence of the power contained in the bag itself and all the medicines it contains shoots into his body. He falls heavily, and lies for a time apparently unconscious.

After a time he quivers, moans, revives, and finally rises to his feet. He addresses the members and tells them that he will now produce from his body the medicine or sacred shell, which is supposed to be the missile of the medicine bag. Retching and groaning he places his hands on his sides, rubbing them slowly upward while he writhes and contorts himself, still retching. His hands reach his shoulders, throat, chin, and mouth, and then the shell (mi'gês, in Sauk) flies into his hands.

Holding the mi'gês in the palm of his hand, he circles the lodge again, showing it to each member, and crying: "Yuhuhuhuhu!" as he does so.

When the leader arrives at his starting point, he claps his hand to his mouth, swallows the shell, and again falls down, unconscious. In a short time he is up again, ejaculating "înî!" to signify that all is in readiness. The attendants now step up to the candidate and throw a blanket over his head, covering his face so that only his eyes can be seen. This is done, it is said, so that the neophyte will not dodge the missile about to be shot into him. The leader now raises the head of his otter bag to the level of his chest, and points it at the candidate. Holding it before him he trots swiftly with pattering feet from the east end of the lodge to the west. Arrived before the neophyte, he blows on the head of his otter and jerks it forward with the medicine cry. The mystic essence contained in the mi'gês is now supposed to shoot into the candidate, who falls unconscious.

The leader now returns to the east and sings this song:

Ni'na nêmishwa'n ni'na.

"I am the one who shot him, I am."

After the fourth repetition, he returns to the west end beside the candidate, and there sings four more songs. Four entire circuits of this nature are made in all. Then he circles the lodge and salutes each member, giving him or her greetings and addressing each by some appropriate term of relationship.

The attendants now strip the candidate (the members were all formerly naked to the waist, it is said, a custom wholly at variance with Menomini and Ojibway ideas, where all are overdressed, if anything), and the garments and also the goods on the sacred ridge pole are handed over to the leader.

Four attempts are now made to raise the candidate who regularly faints, but the last time he is given a revivifying drink called nasä'tcikûn (the reviver) and he comes to life once more.

The leader now takes a pillow on his left arm upon which he strikes a gourd rattle, after shaking it a moment, and, while his assistant accompanies him, carrying the drum, they sing: winapimä winapimi.

All now rise and dance in place, and later the younger members circle the lodge for a half hour's time, all shooting. The candidate is the particular target for his "Uncles and Aunts," who scarcely allow him to rise to his feet, they shoot him so much. He in turn may now use his bag to shoot them.

Finally all sit down again save the Leader, Host, or Master of

Ceremonies, as he may be called, and his assistants. These two officials walk to the east door, turn, and face the west. They sing four songs, then they take the drum to the starting point in the northeast corner, where they beat the drum furiously with cries of "i hê hê," and "i hi hi," "to drive out the Evil Spirit." They then kneel and present the drum and rattle to the next couple on their right, whispering to them to make all possible haste, as the hour is late.

The new pair takes the instruments, circles the lodge regularly, and comes back to the front where they sing their song, making four circuits, after which they return with the drum to the next two members on the right of their starting point, where they pass the drum and rattle on and drop out themselves.

The last couple to receive the drum finishes and carries it to the center of the lodge. All now rise and dance about the circuit, shooting each other promiscuously. An attendant accompanies the candidate to aid and advise him. The candidate is shot down almost continuously, however. At last the drum is carried to the south side—presumably in the southeast corner opposite the starting point, where the dancing and shooting ceases. An intermission of about two hours for feasting follows.

After supper the ceremonies proceed in a similar manner until sundown. At this time the leader takes the members out of the lodge building into the open through the east door and circling it around the north side, all shooting each other promiscuously. This is twice repeated, then all enter the west door, circle the fire in the west (?) end of the structure, and sit down along the sides of the building in their old places for a half hour's rest.

After this, they discuss among themselves who will first enter the sweat lodge, close at hand, which the attendants have meanwhile prepared.

The sweating takes place on the following day, and is regarded as an act of spiritual as well as physical purification. First, that night, the medicine lodge building is torn down by the attendants, as soon as the ceremony is over. The members sleep all night, not rising until about 10 or 11 o'clock on the following day, when the next and last feast is nearly ready.

Young members, of both sexes, accompanied by one old member who is to sing for them, strip themselves naked and enter. A hole is made in the ground in the center of the lodge, and hot stones are placed

therein by the attendants after the covers of the lodge are battened
down tight and the members all present. Mesquite or sagebrush twigs[18]
are thrown on the hot stones as incense, and the leader pours water
on the stones. As the stifling steam rises, he sings twelve sets of four
songs each, and, though they faint, as often happens, from the effect of
the steam, none may leave until it is over.

At length, when the forty-eighth song has been sung, all hastily
leave, and once outside, attendants douse them with pails of cold water.
The ceremony is now concluded with a feast.

Persons are generally initiated to take the place of dead members.
The group which they join provides the initiation fees, except the blanket, which is given by the candidate, and afterwards another is returned to him. All fees go to the leader or initiator.

INSTRUCTIONS GIVEN TO MEDICINE DANCE GUARDS

The leaders of the Medicine Dance were accustomed to instruct
the guards who keep order at the ceremonies as follows, these being
the rules laid down for the informant in 1896 on the occasion of his
first undertaking these duties:

"Let no outsiders come in. Watch the members and see that they
circle the fire before they go out. Keep those who enter circling from
left to right. Keep the spectators back at least ten feet from the lodge,
drive them away from the east door, and herd them to the north as
much as possible, using a long pole to hold them back, regulate the curtain and the lodge covers, see that the drum-heads are tied with rawhide lariats."

PARAPHERNALIA

The articles used by the Sauk during the Medicine Dance are by no
means as varied as those utilized by the other Central Algonkian tribes.
Medicine bags of otter skin, and of the skins of fox squirrels in the
usual rufous, and in melanistic, and albinistic pelage were obtained.
It is said that in former years wolf and bear cub and eagle skins were
also used, but no snake, mink, or weasel skins were seen or heard of.
Besides these, gourd rattles, a modified modern form of the water drum
made from a keg, and the usual cowrie shells are used. The Sauk

---

[18]In their old home they presumably used cedar, as this is still employed
by the northern tribes.

generally thrust colored ribbons through the nostrils of their otter and squirrel-skin bags instead of the colored down used by the other Central Algonkians and Southern Siouans.

A detailed description of the objects used in the Medicine Dance will be given under the heading of Material Culture in another of this series of papers.

CEREMONY ON SELLING AN OTTERSKIN MEDICINE BAG

A fine antique otter-skin medicine bag, ornamented with quill-work in red and yellow, was obtained with two quilled fox squirrel skins from a Sauk named Frank Smith, residing near Shawnee. Mr. Smith, who is one of the leaders of the Medicine Dance, explained that this particular otter was very ancient, having been made in the old Sauk home in Wisconsin. It was his special bag as leader, and was used particularly in the initiation of new members. It was always the first bag to be hung on the ceremonial ridge pole of the lodge, at the eastern end, with its head to the north. It was always likewise the first to be taken down, and was carried on in advance of all others by the leader. It was always the first to be put away in the common receptacle used for the bags of Smith's band after ceremonies, and the last to be taken out of the storage receptacle, when again needed, for the reason that all the rest of the medicine bags were placed on top of it.

When the leader enters the Medicine Lodge structure at the head of his followers at the commencement of the ceremony, the leader stops just inside the east door with his otter in his hand, and there waits until all of his party have entered, the next person to enter being his assistant who carried the drum.

After the candidate has been slain and brought to life again, this bag plays an important part in the promiscuous "shooting" which follows while the drummer keeps up a lively song.

For these reasons, as it was to pass out of the tribe, Smith was particularly anxious to placate the bag before turning it over to the writer, and therefore he addressed a very long and earnest prayer to it, sprinkling Indian tobacco on its head, begging it meanwhile not to be offended, as it was going to a place where it would be far better kept than in his possession, and where it would be cherished forever. Smith presented some tobacco to the writer for use in future sacrifices to the otter, explaining that it was given to the Sauk by Gêtci Mû'nituᵃ, the Great Spirit, and therefore its fumes, when thrown on the fire, were sure to carry messages skyward. Native tobacco is called anên'otäowa sämâ.

THE BUFFALO DANCE

This ceremony is held by the buffalo gens during June or July, this being the time of year when the buffalo shed their hair, or, more rarely, in September when the deer are fat. It is a mimetic rite derived from the bison.

The night before the performance, waiters to the number of eight or ten, chosen from the Bear gens, repair to the appointed place, and make a fire with the bow drill or flint and steel, never with matches. Kettles are put on to boil, dogs are killed, singed, and butchered, while venison, wild turkey, and, especially dedicated to the Buffalo, pumpkins and corn are also boiled. As the food seethes in the kettles the waiters sing from ten to twelve songs, each four times repeated, and these are supposed to last until the food is well cooked. The preparation of the food takes practically all night.

In the morning the rest of the officers and participants in the rite appear. The leader is selected and appointed by the head waiter, and must be a man who on some occasion was the first to take a scalp when out with a war-party. The head waiter invests him with a headdress made of a buffalo scalp with the shiny black horns attached, a buffalo tail is attached to his belt in the rear, an anklet of buffalo dew-claws that tinkle as he moves is attached to his left leg, and a cane or reed whistle is also given him. After the leader, three more men of importance are selected and invested with headdresses made from the heads and horns of domestic steers or cattle. They also wear cowhide necklaces and carry cane whistles, but have no tails or anklets. The fifth person in line is a woman selected because at some time one of her uncles was the first man on a war-party to kill an enemy. After this as many can take part as desire to do so. Mr. Harris has seen as many as twenty dancing.

When all is ready, the drummer gives four sharp strokes on his drum, and the dance commences. The leaders of the participants first whoop, then they blow on their whistles to invoke the buffalo, and all bellow, paw the earth with their feet, and hook at each other in imitation of the animal in whose honor the rite is held. The songs are sung very rapidly, and are in sets of four. The first of these sets is as follows:

1. Hiniwe' tcepasä kwe'ani, kwe'ani!
   "At the place where I got up from."
2. Kina'ne mêtu nikwe'sä
   "I am getting up a dance for you my boy."
3. Patäwenäna kwa'ta
   "I am tasting the (gun) smoke."
4. (a) Tcakemena$^{x'}$ kwatone
      "I am even swallowing all the clouds."
   (b) Tcake näno'sokake
      "All the young buffalo."

Between the sets of songs, the dancers rest. There are three feasts held during the day—at morning, noon, and night. At the concluding set of four songs before each feast, the drum stays are loosened, so that the sound of the strokes become feebler and feebler, and finally die away, then all commence to eat.

The Buffalo Dance was started by a man who was lost and nearly starved to death. The bison took pity on him, fed him, and taught him their dance. They said that the feast at the dance must consist at least in part of vegetables and things that they like to eat. They taught him their medicines, and ordered him to wear the woolly head of a buffalo bull when he led the performance. A buffalo bull was his chief instructor. Spotted domestic cattle also talked to him and instructed him at this time, hence they, too, furnish headdresses for the dance and are included in it.

WOLF GENS CEREMONY

The Wolf gens "owns" what is called Muhwä'wûk Winimîtcikäwûk, or the "Wolves Give Their Dance," also known as the "Summer Dance of the Wolf." This is a religious feast not connected with any other. All the gens bundles are present and open, and the bundle owners fast all day till night, when they are given a special feast, which does not, however, include dog meat. Some of the songs are as follows:

Nêwi nêwi täma, nêku'te tcämosa.
"I am going with one mate,"

This song refers to one of the characteristics of the wolf, which, say the Sauk, is a strictly monogamous animal.

Hanikwa'ya ma'nêtuwiwa.

"Squirrel skin has a great spirit in it."

The informant stated that this song refers to the private war medicine of a member of the Wolf gens. He heard it sung when the Sauk were paying a visit to the Osage, and the individual in question desired to be well received and obtain many presents. He, therefore, called upon his guardian, the squirrel, to help him "charm the enemy," i. e., the Osage. The informant added that personal guardian songs of this type belonging to members of the Wolf gens were sung at the Wolf gens ceremony.

SMOKING PONIES, OR ANOHIWÊTIWATC

When a visit was being paid to another tribe, the first gens to lead the pilgrims was generally the Fish. Five or six miles would be covered, and then the tribe would camp, and the next day some other gens would take the lead, changing each day. On the last day when within three or four miles of the tribe which was to be their host, two Ki'shko and two Oskû'sh were sent over to the strangers to announce the arrival of the Sauk. These heralds carried with them a few scraps of calico and some tobacco to show that their people were bringing presents, and each also carried a red stone pipe. The messengers would deliver their messages, talk, and smoke, until a place to camp was assigned for the Sauk by their hosts. Then, accompanied by one of the host tribe as a guide, they would return, and as the Sauk proceeded, a large party of the other people would intercept them on the way to receive the gifts they had brought.

On their arrival the Sauk would go into camp, and then their hosts would feast them and set a time three or four days ahead for the return of the gifts. The first night and the next morning after their arrival there would be a big dance, a so-called "war dance," and this might be kept up as much as two days before the return presents were made.

When the great day arrived, the host tribe started early in the afternoon, after an hour's work they stopped and passed the pipe. On such occasions it did not even have to be lighted, or to possess a bowl. This seems to be an idea derived from the calumet ceremonies of the Southern Siouan tribes, where the pipe stem in such matters is all important.

If the pipe stem was offered to a man, it meant the gift of a horse. If the stranger meant to give a blanket only, he came and shook hands. Sometimes instead of passing the pipe, sticks were given out, each representing a horse. The writer has himself seen this done by the Menomini at the Dream Dance.

After the distribution of the presents there was one more farewell dance, and then the visitors returned.

THE DREAM DANCE, GHOST DANCE, PEYOTE

This ceremony, of the Central Algonkian form, is beginning to die out. One of the great drums was offered for sale to the writer. The Ghost Dance, though said to have been prevalent among the Ioway and Pawnee, did not affect the Sauk.

Peyote has strong vogue, and occurs in a semi-Christian type.

CONDUCT OF FEASTS

The night or day before any feast or before any ceremony involving a feast, the waiters or servants gather at the place appointed and prepare the food that is to be served, tidy the spot, and put everything to rights. When all the guests have arrived, each waiter takes a bundle of short sticks or reeds called pamakwo'mîkwûnûn, "measuring, or scoring, sticks," and goes out and hands one to each member of his moiety present as an invitation to come and eat, each stick representing a piece of meat in the kettles, there being one or more bundles of sticks for each variety of food offered. When the guests come in, the Master of Ceremonies or host, who takes no part in the feast, makes a speech of dedication and welcome placing tobacco on the fire. It is his function to do all the singing and speaking for the occasion.

When the food is duly dedicated, it is served, while the Master of Ceremonies sings, and the representatives of the moieties eat in contest. The waiters collect the sticks from the guests as they are served. When all the food has been portioned out, the guests eat, and the waiters start to prepare more food.

At each of the four corners of the lodge are guards or officials who are called gäkinawatû'pijîk who represent the four mythical serpents who uphold the four corners, north, east, south, and west, of the earth island. They do nothing but smoke during the rites.

The waiters themselves are entitled to eat the head, feet, and brisket of each dog killed.

After the feast is over, the waiters gather the bones together in a pile in the east corner of the lodge—by the "east post," while the sticks are bundled together. The bones are then carried 100 yards or more to the east of the place and there cast away.

Sometimes, in the case of the Feast of the Dead (Tci'bä Ku'kwän) the bones are saved till night and then burned. At this feast, instead of having individual wooden bowls, each invited guest bringing his own, four or five people eat out of one large bowl, and some meat is thrown in the fire for the dead.

ORDER OF FEAST SERVICE

In the Medicine Lodge ceremonies and all other sacred functions, the food used for feasting is dedicated, by the Master of Ceremonies or Leader, to the Gods in the order of their importance, as follows:

First, a kettle of singed and boiled dog to the Great Spirit, Gêtci Mû'nito[a].[19]

Second, a portion of the food to Wi'sakä.

Third, a portion of the food is set aside for the Thunderers.

Fourth, all birds are dedicated to the Water Spirits (snakes and panthers). Pumpkins are the perquisite of the buffalo, and sweets of the bear.

FEAST OF THANKSGIVING FOR THE CROPS, OR THE GREEN CORN DANCE

This ceremony was called Nipäniwithêniwîn or Summer Food Feast, and was held every year before the people commenced to eat vegetables from their gardens. The feast was given successively by the different gentes, first the Fish gens, then the Ocean, Thunder, Bear, and Buffalo, etc., the Wolf gens coming last.

The host, who was generally the chief of the gens, gave a talk and thanked the Great Spirit for the corn, beans, melons and other garden products, and for His ever present help. Indian tobacco, called "The Messenger of the Gods" by the Sauk, was used for incense. The people who had been fasting, then washed the charcoal from their faces, and

---

[19]Dogs were killed by giving them food and clubbing them while eating it, as none of their blood should be shed.

all the members of the gens might eat fresh vegetables without stint from then on.

After the Wolf gens had had its feast, it was customary in the old days for the warriors of that body to shave their heads. It was not possible for them to do so otherwise without giving a special feast. Tradition states that the other gentes formerly made this requirement of their warriors, but that the custom was abandoned.

FALL FEAST AND FALL HUNT

In the fall a feast called Tukwagikigä'nowîn was held, in order that the hunters might be successful. After this, in October, the families separated and scattered throughout the forest. The old people stayed behind all winter to keep the house and goods. In modern times at least, the hunting lasted four months, the people returning in March to trade their furs.

NIGHT FEAST

The name of this ceremony, Ninipap'iwûk, means "Sitting up all night." It is held in a bark house of the usual large square type. The east and west doors are guarded by female officials called Manitu'-okwä'ûg, or "Serpent Woman," who guard against the entrance of evil spirits. Old women are always selected for this office.

At intervals the dancers get down from one scaffold which flanks the north and south walls of the ordinary Sauk house (for sleeping and sitting purposes) face each other, and dance in position, occasionally whooping. In the center of the floor near one end is a spot (altar) dedicated to Skutänä'siⁿ or "The Fire Keeper" and another devoted to the moon, Tepä'ki-gi'shûs (night sun) the patron of the rites. A banner, bearing a representation of the moon upon it, is raised in the center of the camp.

Certain men who attend are seated one at each corner of the house. The sacred bundles of the gens giving the ceremony are all opened and displayed facing the fire, but at dawn they are closed, the flag taken in, and the ceremony ended.

THE BARK HOUSE FEAST AND WINTER QUARTERS FEAST

When a new bark house was built, the sacred bundles or mi'shâmᵃⁿ, were first moved in, and then a feast was given before the family could occupy it. After the feast the bundles and the invitation sticks were hung up and then the people came in to stay. It is also said that the entire village could not change from summer to winter quarters or vice versa without first holding a feast. After this the bark houses could be patched up, and the people could move in.

TYPES OF SHAMANS

Sisa'ki'eûk: These are "Doctors" who ascertain what ails their patients by making a small cylindrical house of poles and bark which they enter and then call upon the Underworld Spirits, especially the snakes and turtle, to aid them. The spectators can hear the doctor calling upon his familiars by name, for in addition to snapping turtle, who is the principal helper of this class of seers, the following manitous are also invoked:

Kwägwäshiwä°, the Chief Underworld Serpent.

Mä'sakomigo'kwä°, our Grandmother, the Earth.

Wi'sakä, the Culture Hero.

Shawa'natäsiu, the Southern God.

As the various deities invoked arrive at the conjuror's lodge, the onlookers hear them land on the floor within with a flop. Then the doctor is heard to inquire: "When will my patient get well?" The answer will be, "She will get well (or die, as the case may be) in four days." It may be that the crisis will be reached in less time if the doctor is very powerful, but it cannot take longer. After some further conversation the visiting manitous may call for a pipe to smoke, so a huge pipe is filled and lighted and shoved into the tent from beneath by relatives of the patient. It will be smoked to the end in an instant. Finally the spirits leave, but, although they go out as they came in, through the roof of the structure, they are invisible. The doctor comes out by raising the covering and crawling forth beneath it.

Sometimes in order to show his power the doctor will allow himself to be tightly bound before commencing his performance. Men will take thongs and tie his arms above the elbows and behind his back and thus thrust him into his lodge, yet he will succeed in untying himself almost immediately, and the ropes will come hurtling out of the lodge.

Doctors of this class can also cause the winds to blow while they are at work. They are also the practitioners who suck out disease with bone tubes, and make incisions with flint chips and bleed the patient with a cupping horn.

One of the practices of the Sisa'ki'eûk is divination by the use of a powder. A quarter of a teaspoonful of pulverized root medicine of some secret sort is taken and thrown in a wooden bowl full of water. If it all floats in a single mass in the center the patient will recover, if it sinks, the patient will die. In such a case the fees paid in advance for the divination and treatment are returned. The doctor makes no further attempt to cure.

Wä^{x}kaji'hûk: These are doctors of a different class from those just described. They have the power to slap their hands on the earth and shoot evil into a person. These men meet in public contests in which they vie with one another to run through fires, throw hot ashes at each other, etc., while they bellow like buffaloes. If there is any food boiling on the fire they strive to see who can snatch it out of the kettle and eat it without being scalded. They have certain songs that, when sung, render them invulnerable. It is said that the people were more afraid of these doctors than they were of witches in former days, saying of them, "They are like ghosts." However, these men, unlike the witches, who performed in secret, did all their rites openly.

From the foregoing descriptions it can be plainly seen that these two classes of doctors correspond with the "Je'sako" or "Jesakaid," and "Wabano" cults of the other Central and Northern Algonkian tribes.

Manitu'-we'siu are human beings who practice witchcraft, turning themselves into various animals, such as bears, fowls, dogs, wolves, turkeys, or owls in order to accomplish the destruction of their enemies by means of black magic. This is a very common belief among all the Central Algonkians, Southern Siouans and even the Iroquois and Algonkian tribes of the east.

GAMES

Lacrosse: This game, called Pâgaha'toän, was the great athletic sport of the Sauk in former times, but has now fallen largely into desuetude. It was customary for one village or one band to play against another, the "Poker Players" against the "Dry Bones" for example. On one occasion, the informant remembers that when there was a dispute over the ownership of fourteen head of cattle, it was settled by having the contesting parties play a game of ball with the cattle as a prize. The tribal moieties of Ki'shko and Oskú'sh did not figure in such games except in minor games held in the same village.

Before commencing a game the ball sticks were collected from the players and shuffled, then they were matched in parallel rows, as is still done among the Menomini. They were then counted by the Braves, who saw to it that the sides were equal in number and who threw out the odd man, if there was one. The actual number of players did not matter so long as the numbers were balanced. These rules and the method of selecting players also apply to the woman's shinny game.

The ball was thrown up in the center of the field, and the first side to score four goals won. The goals were from 200 yards to a quarter of a mile apart. The man who throws the ball for the players had to be a Brave and a member of the Ki'shko division. Before tossing it in the air he counted a coup, saying, for example: "I brought home a Commanche head, and that is the way you should bring home a trophy now!" He whooped and threw the ball, whereupon all the players whooped and charged for it. There had to be two mounted men on each side to urge on and encourage the players. The winners gave their prizes, of cloth, etc., as a rule, to their nieces.

Woman's Shinny Game: The rules of this game and the manner of playing it are very similar to the man's game of Lacrosse. It is called Ko'nûnohûk and is played with a double ball and a straight stick. The women divide according to moiety, and the prizes when distributed are given to the uncles of the winners. In this game the prizes are generally sacks of flour.

Arrow Shooting Contest: Archery contests, Aia'wîtcihiwatc, were held in the spring, the men dividing moiety against moiety. Two small sticks about the thickness of a finger and a yard in length were peeled, and set up close together across a hollow about one hundred yards in width. The contestants, standing on the opposite side of the hollow, tried to score eleven points. To shoot an arrow between the two sticks counted one, to hit either stick counted two, to split a stick counted five. Deer antler points were used. Horses, saddles, and guns were bet upon the outcome.

Bowl and Dice: This is a woman's game, called Ko'ˣsikäwin. A knot bowl and eight dice, six round, and two carved like thunderbirds or turtles, made of antler or bone, white on one side and dark on the other, are used. The winning score is eleven points, but the count differs with different individuals.

Moccasin Game: The native term for this play is Papano'tcihiwîn Mamakäsähi'wûn, or "Long Distance Moccasin Game." The players, four on a side, are set twenty-five or thirty feet apart. One man being called over each time to guess. The guesser strikes at the moccasin wherein he thinks the bullet is concealed with an elk-horn quirt. If he gets it right he scores four points, if he fails he loses four. There are eight points to the game. The winner of a guess takes the moccasins back over to his side. Each side has two drummers and singers who try to distract the attention of their opponents by singing funny songs, mostly obscene, such as: "Black Testicles;" or, when playing against the Mûskwaki', "Kenaponaiya asian," which means "Breech clout in front, bare back." The songs are often of this nature, twitting upon the personal or tribal peculiarities of the other side.

Moccasin was often played against members of some visiting tribe, such as the Ioway.

Ice Game: The implements used in this game, called Mêshkwä'pi, of which each player has two, are slender hickory wands about a yard long, with heavy swollen heads. These can be thrown over smooth ice to a distance of half a mile. Betting is heavy, and twenty consecutive points must be scored. The moieties, as usual, play against each other, and sometimes the game is played tribe against tribe, the Ioway being frequent rivals.

EXPLANATION OF PLATE I.

Rev. William Harris, Sauk interpreter.

BULLETIN

OF THE

PUBLIC MUSEUM OF THE CITY OF MILWAUKEE

Vol. 5, No. 2, pp. 59–95, Plates 2–12   May 11, 1925

Observations on the Ethnology of the Sauk Indians

Part II, WAR CUSTOMS

By

Alanson Skinner

Observations on the Ethnology of the Sauk Indians

Part II, War Customs

CONTENTS

ILLUSTRATIONS

INTRODUCTION

As all the Central Algonkian and Southern Siouan tribes derived a great part of their sustenance from the chase, they required a large territory for their range. Such a district they were able to maintain only through the force of arms. Else it would have been overrun by their neighbors and the game supply materially decreased. Thus, in order to protect themselves against encroachment, each adult male was of necessity a warrior, prepared either to resist intrusion or to invade, and, as raids led to counterstrokes and reprisals, every tribe was often in a more or less continuous state of war with one or more of its neighbors. War for the mere conquest of new territory was rare or even unknown.

The fickle character of the natives, their lack of a sense of cohesion, the nature of the country itself and the uncertainty of the food supply, made standing armies impossible. There was no such general military organization as found among the Iroquois and perhaps some other more eastern tribes. A sort of guerrilla warfare was carried on by temporary volunteer parties, seldom of large size. As rewards in the way of insignia and public recognition were granted successful warriors, warfare became a game with certain more or less fixed rules. Indeed, it was the greatest of all gambling games, for in it one man staked his life against that of another, growing great in the eyes of his own people in ratio to the number of war honors or scalps that he wrested from his foes, while his own scalplock was cultivated both to wave defiance at the enemy, and to reward with a tangible trophy the foeman who was man enough to slay him.

To some extent the old methods were changed with the introduction of firearms and the growing encroachment of the whites. War became more deadly, more people were killed in battle, and the enforced migration of whole nations brought on desperate struggles for mere existence. Often, too, one tribe was set against another for reasons of white policy. Moreover, in many cases, the white-men themselves appeared as a new enemy, and although they were less formidable in some respects than the native peoples, who combined the forest lore of wild animals with the intelligence of men, they were immensely formidable because of their incomprehensible numbers. What opportunity indeed had a native American tribe, numbering a paltry few thousand souls, however brave or skilled, against the steady influx of hordes of whites with the incalculable numbers of Europe behind them, and armed with the most modern weapons of destruction?

Except for a certain ferocity and aggressiveness, rare among Indians of the Algonkian stock, the Sauk closely resembled their neighbors in all the foregoing matters. From the earliest known times however, their truculent spirit involved them in difficulties. Their entire history up to recent years has been one of continuous warfare and enforced migration, for with all their martial ardor they suffered defeat after defeat, and, while esteemed for their bravery by most of their enemies, they have never been able to hold their own against their foes for any length of time. Their fate was largely shared by the Meskwaki or Foxes, their kindred and ancient allies, from whom they have been for some time estranged, but with this people the present paper has no dealings.

Among the earliest records of Sauk history is the tradition of their expulsion from Saginaw, Michigan, by the Ojibway, in prehistoric times. There is considerable evidence that they once lived still farther east, and were forced to Michigan by the Iroquois. We next find them domiciled on the Door County peninsula of Green Bay, Wisconsin, whence again they were driven by a related Algonkian tribe, the Menomini. That the Sauk were forced from Michigan by the numerous Ojibway is not surprising, but their overthrow by the Menomini, who were certainly no greater in numbers, and decidedly less belligerent in disposition, is somewhat remarkable. Next we find the Sauk and the Foxes involved in war with the French and again defeated by the whites and their Menomini allies. They were once more driven from their seats near the west shore of Green Bay inland to the Mississippi, in northwestern Illinois and southwestern Wisconsin. Here, though at war with the Illinois and Pawnee, the greater part of the Sauk still dwelt up to the time of the Black Hawk War, in 1832. In this new location they battled on the north with the Santee Dakota, who still admire their individual prowess, and also with the Comanche on the south. After the Black Hawk war, the story of which is too well known to need repetition here, ended in their final overthrow by the United States troops, aided again by the Menomini, the Sauk withdrew to Kansas, and, except for Kwaskami's band, eventually were removed to Oklahoma, where they are still to be found.

In spite of their lust for fighting, the Sauk, like all the other Central tribes, were an intensely religious people, who believed that no one could succeed in any undertaking without divine or supernatural help of some kind. This help, in the case of warfare, was vested in certain portable shrines, or war bundles, which were carried to, but seldom in, battle.

SACRED BUNDLES

While all bundles of a sacred sort are called by the Sauk mi'shâm, plural mi'shâman (equivalent to the Menomini pe'tcikunau, petcikuna'tian), the proper name for the war bundle is natopa'ni mi'shâm, or "war-sacred-bundle." (See plate II, fig. 2.) Unlike the Menomini war bundles, which are strictly personal property, Sauk bundles, although claimed and operated by individuals, belong to the gens. The so-called "naming" or "namesake" bundles are said to be really a variety of war bundle which is opened when a man's name is changed in the field because of an exploit on the warpath, "so that men may hear and know." The partizan always has the right to take a new name before the rest of his men.

The chieftainship of each gens of the Sauk was hereditary in the leading families, the chief always being the eldest lineal male descendant of the gens ancestor. Each chief in later times was custodian of the sacred war bundles of his gens, which, though formerly kept by private individuals, are now stored in a separate bark house set aside for that purpose. In this repository the rest of the gens' ceremonial articles, such as rattles, invitation sticks, and the like, are also stored. When the eldest descendant of the chief was a woman, it was customary to transmit her title and the gens properties, such as the war bundles, to her younger brother or her nearest male relative in the gens.

Generally, bundles were given to young men after the end of the puberty fast, by their relatives, who presented the bundles to them even if they had not dreamed concerning war powers. In this manner Mê'siwûk received his. When, however, a man had dreamed the right to have a bundle, it was made up according to the instructions given him in his dream. As a matter of theory, only such individuals as had dreamed the right could own war bundles, whereas actually, it is said, every head of a household had one or more. These often came to him either by gift after his puberty fast and consequent assumption of manhood, or by inheritance from deceased relatives of his own gens, but never, so far as could be learned, by purchase. When a bundle owner dies today and there are no near relatives in his gens to take over the shrine, it remains in the gens ceremonial bark house and is cared for by the chief or an officer appointed by the gens council for that purpose.

Among the war bundles was a special variety called the "Charging Bundle" or mai'nake mi'shâm. These are miniature war bundles which are tied to the belt on the left side and worn over the left hip when charging, whereas, with ordinary mishâ'man, the partizan stays behind "making medicine" and does not take active part in the battle himself. The warriors, when using a charging bundle, discard all other clothing, even the breech-cloth, because the bundle magically serves both for protection and garment. Two of these belonging to the Wolf gens were obtained from Austen Grant. One shown in plate II, fig. 1, holds a duck-hawk and a few amulets in a skin-tight envelope of deer hide. It was said to have been a partizan's talisman, and was especially used in leading forlorn hope attacks. Usually, however, while very small, these bundles are miniatures of the larger type, and are complete with representative paraphernalia, for the idea was to compress all the powers of a regular mi'shâm into small compass and thus get greater protection than if carrying a single charm. In the case of the hawk bundle, above described, the bird was faced towards the foe before attacking, and its bearer said, "Now we are going after your meat!" If he himself was the first to take a scalp, after the return, he would stop the drummer in the midst of the scalp dance and announce, "My hawk has fed his brothers. He has laid so many bodies on the ground for the Almighty Crow." Then the bearer would make a present to the four singers of tobacco or a dog, the latter being for them to eat.

The charging bundle of the Bear gens is said to be a wildcat skin used as a belt, split so that the head is worn in front. On this account the members of the Bear gens never kill wildcats.

WAR PARTIES

War parties were made up of volunteers under a bundle owner who acted as their leader or partizan. Sometimes all the members of the war party were of one gens, but frequently several gentes were involved. The united warriors of the entire tribe seldom, if ever, went out at one time, as, for example, among the Iroquois. In some instances more than one bundle was carried, in which case that of the gens chief took precedence. At other times the partizan carried only selected medicines and amulets from his bundle, and not the entire shrine. Old and renowned warriors, who had had much success as partizans, and whose bundles were credited with correspondingly great powers, usually drew to them large numbers of young men who aspired to social elevation through reputation for military prowess.

After word had been sent through the community that a war party was about to take the field, the warriors would gather under their leaders at some appointed place, where a council was held and the possibility of "hunting for the enemy" and "finding one or two scalps" was discussed. If all were agreed, a feast was made a few days later and sacrifices offered for victory. Each warrior was equipped with war club and knife, for although bow and arrows were frequently taken, they were not considered indispensable, especially as greater credit redounded to a man who killed an enemy in hand-to-hand conflict than to one who shot a foe at a distance. Each also carried several pairs of moccasins, if the way was to be long, and a deerskin bag containing pounded parched corn, dried meat, and maple sugar, mixed in equal parts and weighing two to five pounds. This was carried in his belt, and was his only ration, a very little sufficing for a meal. If any warrior lacked personal or horse equipment, he was usually able to borrow it, but, it is said, could impress what he needed, if the owner was not willing to lend it.

In olden times the war party set out on foot for the enemy's country, but more recently the men departed mounted on horseback. The partizan went ahead, leaving several hours before the rest, attended by two or three servants, who were often his nephews. He bore the bundle on his chest between him and the enemy, in order that its power might protect the party and on the return, for the same reason, carried it on his back. He was obligated not to lay it down, or to turn back or step aside, although if a change of course was absolutely necessary, his own nephew or uncle might take him by the shoulders and turn him. An uncle or nephew of the partizan might at any time go to him and take the bundle from him, after which he had the privilege of changing course at will. However, any deviations from the straight path were considered unlucky, and the warriors usually tried to start out on the open prairie, where trees or streams were not likely to interfere with their going.

According to Galland, if the departing warriors happened to meet a member of their own people while still within their own tribal boundaries, he was treated to a severe beating unless he was a runner on an errand, or himself returning from a war excursion. Each member of the war party would strike him with his ramrod, arrow, or some other weapon as he passed. This the unfortunate man was obliged to stand and receive quietly, "as a tax levied upon him by his country men for protecting him and his family from the common enemy."

At nightfall the party went into camp, usually making their beds in a circle or hollow square. The partizan and his seasoned warriors smoked and talked while the fresh recruits made the evening meal by mixing the pounded corn with water in the proportion of an ounce to a pint of liquid, unless far from hostile ground, as they dared not make a fire when near the enemy lest they be discovered. All are said to have eaten out of the same bowl with the same spoon. When the war party was at a greater distance from the foe, the young men sometimes cooked a meal for the warriors. Each partizan was accompanied by servants from the gens or gentes which bore reciprocal functions with his own. These men cooked for him, and, if the party was mounted, cared for his horse. Youths, on their first warpath, never sat down or slept in the presence of their superiors, and did sentry duty at night, posting their own guards. When the older warriors were sleeping the recruits formed an outer circle, within the ring of sentinels, and slept there, relieving those on watch from time to time.

When a war party had been gone for four days, the women of the home camp would race out a half mile in the direction that the party had taken, there halt, throw tobacco after the warriors and make speeches, of which the following was given the writer as a sample:

"My uncle, hold fast to your gun, and don't drop your sacred bundle."

After this, the women would whoop and race back to the village. The winner, it was thought, would cause her uncle to count first coup, the most coveted war honor.

When camp was made, on the second or third day out, the warriors would sing boastful songs about what they were going to do, and, at the conclusion of each song, call out the name of their bundle owner. After three or four days of travel, the war party would halt for a day and a night. If they were but a few miles from the enemy, two men were sent out as scouts to observe whether or not the enemy's camp was well guarded, and the best way to approach it without being seen. The scouts were expected to be gone from half a day to a day or more.

When the partizan began to think it time for the return of his scouts, he would take his mi'shâm and, facing the direction whence he expected them to come, he would lay it crosswise in front of him. The scouts, if they had seen the foe, would return on the run and spring over the bundle feigning to walk on the partizan, thus letting the war party know that they had seen the enemy and at the same time taking oath, according to custom, that what they were about to tell would be the truth. Else the mi'shâm would bring disaster on their heads.

As the scouts stepped over the bundle, they would exclaim, "We have seen elk feeding along," or "We have seen buffallo grazing," which was a set formula for announcing that they had discovered the enemy. The variety of animal symbolizing the foe apparently being chosen to correspond with the gens of the speakers. The partizan would ejaculate "Henêkohe'," or "All right," and at once another war council would be held to decide the particulars of the attack. The rest of the day and night would be spent in preparing, and for three or four hours war songs would be sung. These songs, of course, were parts of the bundle ritual. Then they would wait until nearly dawn when the partizan and his waiters or assistants would sing a short but important song intended to lull the fears of the unsuspecting foe and cause them to sleep more soundly. Then the partizan remained behind, with his bundle open on the earth before him, and sang and conducted the ceremonies while his men,who carried amulets (see plates VII to IX), from the bundle, went mounted or on foot and attacked the camp of the foe. The signal for the charge was given with the reed war whistles, which were usually attached to the outside of each bundle.

A typical song sung by the partizan while the attack was commencing was collected with a war bundle of the Deer gens from an old Sauk named "Jesse James," Mamiâ'shikum or "Ugly Nose," of the Deer clan, who resided near Avery, Oklahoma. It ran, four times repeated:

"Mai'näpano tûkwûnosa motcikänâmokumî ki' heha piyani."

It is said to mean, "Die on the surface of the ground, you will be under the earth some day."

As might be expected, the war customs of the various gentes differed slightly from each other. A war bundle, differing from all the others obtained or seen, was collected from the Bear-potato gens. This war bundle formerly belonged to an old man named originally Apwä'osä, "Walking-in-a-pack," of the Wolf clan. This man was later adopted into the Bear-potato clan, and was given the name (or nickname?) of Tci'katu, or "Coffee pot," and was awarded custody of the bundle. He died in 1889, and the bundle was purchased from Franklin Harding, one of his descendants, who resided near Cushing, Oklahoma.

As usual, the bundle has an outer wrapper of tanned deer skin to which are attached a pair of cane whistles. Inside are the skins of two otters, shown in plate IV, a large one and a small one, both stuffed with native tobacco. To the larger otter (fig. 1) are attached no less than eighteen fragments of human scalps or wisps of human hair, representing scalps taken from the enemy. To the smaller otter (fig. 2) are attached eight similar scalps. These are fastened to the head, in the neighborhood of the mouth, and to the feet of these animals with sinew threads. The tails are apparently missing. There is also a stick carved like a human mentula, to which are attached three wisps of human hair. This stick with the scalplocks is said to represent old men taken prisoner by the Bear-potato clan war parties. There are also four forked sticks and two straight cross pieces to make a small rack upon which the otter skins were supported when the bundle was opened. Nothing else occurs in the bundle with the exception of a few feathers dyed red which seem to have been at one time attached to a war pipe.

In war parties of the Bear-potato gens, when the scouts were expected back, near the hour of dawn, the partizan set the four forked sticks in the ground in the form of a rectangle. He removed the sod for about two square feet, the area covered by the rectangle outlined by the sticks, so that the earth was bare. He squatted behind this, and set up the small rods with the otters lying upon them, their heads somewhat raised and pointing in the direction of the enemy, "for otters, when on the watch, lie with their heads a little higher than their bodies." The sharpened sticks which accompany the rack, and the wooden mentula, were stuck in the ground slanting towards the enemy. There should be in the bundle a plaited potato vine strand of six or eight strings braided together which the partizan should wear as a symbol of his gens, and it was said by my informants that the bundle of each gens should have a talisman of some material representing its symbolic animal or object.

As the partizan awaited the return of the scouts, he untied a package of native tobacco and made it ready, holding some loose in his hand. As the scouts came in Indian file, walking fast, they held their bows with the arrows strung, toward the enemy's camp. They stepped over the shrine, and the partizan exclaimed: "Henêkohe'," while the scouts remarked, (if they discovered the enemy asleep) "We saw a big pile of potatoes heaped together in one place."

The partizan now commenced sprinkling tobacco on the four stakes and on the otters, beginning at the tails and working forward to the heads. He dug a little hole in the center of the square plot beneath the grill and placed tobacco there for Masakumigo'kwä°, "Our Grandmother," the earth. He covered this and then spoke and told his men that they would attempt an early morning attack about dawn, when human vitality is at its lowest ebb. He then begged Our Grandmother, the earth, for help. While the fight was going on, similar prayers were repeated by the leader, who stayed behind with the bundle, and when the warriors returned with their scalps, the usual ceremonies of name changing and the like were held. After the return home, the scalp dance was held and a wisp of hair taken from each scalp was tied on one of the otters.

Warriors of the Bear-potato gens, when in action, wore only their belts and leggings, and no breech-cloths. Indeed, this custom was apparently general, for the Sauk believe that should one of their number be killed and his ceremonial clothes fall into the hands of the enemy, the whole nation would soon suffer disaster. In general, the breech-cloths found in the bundles (see plate VI) were worn in front when charging and in back while retreating, "to be between the wearer and the foe." The warriors carried their knives on their belts at their backs, and their quivers were bound tight to the left side, the mouths being near their arm pits, and not over the shoulder, in the way they were carried for hunting. In drawing the bow, the first and second fingers were used to pull back the string.

Should the scouts not see an enemy, they did not return in a straight line, but circled around on the right side, coming in on the left of the partizan. Often such a failure sent back the war party as ill omened. When this happened, all came home weeping. The scouts when deployed on their business, signalled to each other with cries of owls, or wolves, and it is said in derision by the Sauk, that the Osage, when scouting, cried like quails even though it was in the night.

PRISONERS

When the warriors returned from a raid, their captives were bound with prisoner ties which are found in many bundles as shown in plate IX, figs. 1-3. These are called t'sûpap when made of plaited Indian hemp, and when made of leather thongs, pisha'gûn. They are often ornamented with porcupine quill tassels. The prisoner's arms were folded behind his back and tied fast with rope at the elbows, while another, usually light and ornamental, was placed around his neck to lead him by, his captor going in advance shaking a gourd rattle and singing. The method of tying captives and the hempen ties themselves strongly suggest Iroquois or other eastern influences. When a successful war party neared the home village, that is, when the warriors were about three-quarters of a mile away, those who had taken scalps or captives would whoop "Ho hau! Ho hau!" At once all those who had stayed behind would race to the spot, the first four to touch the scalps or the captives being allowed to count coup. Sometimes a scalp was given to the first to touch it, especially if it was a woman who won the race. A custom somewhat similar to this was once found among the Menomini.

Although consistently accused of atrocities by other Central tribes, the Sauk deny that they ever tortured their prisoners. It is true that adult males were seldom taken captive, as they were not likely to accept the conditions of captivity, and were dangerous to their captors. They were generally slain at once. Young men or women were presented to the chief or to famous warriors and the males were kept as slaves to chop wood or attend to their persons, light their pipes, etc. Women or young girls became the wives of the chief or partizan. Apparently the captor did not keep his prisoners himself, under any circumstances, but always gave them to his superior officers in the gens. Young boys were brought up as slaves, but when grown, were given presents of clothes, etc., and then allowed to choose whether they would join the tribe of their captor or go back to their own people. It is said that insubordinate slaves were turned over to the warriors for execution. It is certain that among all the Central tribes, the treatment of captives was infinitely milder even at its worst than among other tribes of the east, particularly the Iroquois.

WAR HONORS

The first four warriors to count coup upon an enemy in battle were entitled to have their names changed at once by the partizan in charge, without further ceremony, providing only that some name "belonging" to the gens of the bearer was used. The man who actually killed an enemy or scalped him was entitled to wear jinglers or bells on his moccasins and scalp-fringed leggings at ceremonies and councils.

A pair of deerskin leggings was obtained from a Sauk named Albert Moore, who had been a soldier in the late World War, and who was reputed to have killed several of the enemy. In addition to fringe and tassels, he wore small bells attached to his leggings.

Each of the four men who counted coup on an enemy and were thus entitled to change their names, were also given the right to wear an eagle feather for each exploit (see plate III, figs. 2-5), but war bonnets of the type common among the Sioux, Cheyenne, and other Plains tribes, were never used. The native title for a brave is Watâ'sä°, and a similar term survives as a personal name in Menomini.

Coups were also counted by the first four men or women, to race out from the village and touch each scalp and prisoner brought home by the war party. Galland[1] gives some interesting data on the subject of war honors. He says: "This rule also obtains in war; he who wounds or kills an enemy, has a right to the scalp, but if another strike him with his hand before the first does, he is not only entitled to wear the painted hand upon his robe blanket, but also to the spoils taken from the body of the fallen foe."

SCALP DANCE

After the return of a war party, the scalp dance or mi'sê^{x}kwe^i was held, the whole community—men, women, and children taking part. In it each warrior showed his trophies, sang songs lauding himself, recounted his deeds in detail at intervals, and called himself by the new name he had earned by his bravery, while boasting of his prowess. One of these songs connected with one of the principal bundles of the Wolf gens is simply: Pa'toka n'ma'yaha', "Comanche, I made him cry."

A typical boast, heard from Rev. Wm. Harris, was: "In this manner I shot him down! He cried out and begged for mercy, but I had no pity for him, he was my enemy!"

After the coup counting, an eating race was held between four selected warriors from each of the moieties of the tribe, Oskû'sh and Ki'shko.

---

[1]Galland, Dr. Isaac, "The Indian Tribes of the West," The Annals of Iowa, Vol. VII, No. 3, p. 275.

COUP COUNTING AT ADOPTION FEASTS

At adoption feasts braves were sometimes chosen to take the place of dead warriors. At such a time all the accredited braves of the tribe, regardless of gens or moiety, were invited. All sat in a row and beat upon a wooden bowl instead of a drum for their music. The first one in line would rise and count his coups, dramatizing his deeds, and concluding with a well known saying that was called "Feeding the Raven," Kakakiu wisê^{n}iu, and consisted of the words: "At this time I fed the Almighty Crow on human flesh." Then all would dance, after which another would rise and speak.

In the Buffalo gens a man who counted first coup was given a buffalo tail to wear at the scalp dance. In the Turkey gens the prized trophy was an ornamented deerskin breech-clout. Sometimes plain or scarlet dyed eagle plumes with quilled shaft ornaments were awarded.

NAMES OF ENEMY TRIBES

	Singular	Plural
Comanche	Pa'toka	(hûk)
Sioux	Asha'	(hûk)
Menomini	Mûno'mîne	(kajîk)

ORIGIN OF THE SACRED BUNDLES

Mr. M. R. Harrington, in his paper entitled "Sacred Bundles of the Sac and Fox Indians,"[2] gives a lengthy myth, purporting to account for the origin of these shrines among the Sauk. This he obtained from the late Mêshê'bêkwa, who was at that time the keeper of the Wolf Gens Bundle House near Cushing, Oklahoma. The tale relates the fasting and adventures of a man named Pitoshkah', who was said to have been the first to receive a sacred war bundle from the Powers Above. Later, Mr. Harrington's assistant, William Skye, a Peoria Indian, collected a variant of the same myth. Curiously enough, the present writer was unable to obtain any confirmation of this story. Without exception all the Sauk with whom he conversed upon the subject, including the late Austen Grant, son of Mêshê'-bêkwa, who had succeeded his father in charge of the Wolf Gens Bundle House, declared that they had never heard any such legend,

---

[2]Anthropological Publications, University Museum, Univ. Penn., Vol. IV, No. 2, Phila., 1914.

adding that the first bundle came to the tribe through the Culture Hero, Wi'sakä, who obtained it by tricking Turtle, as is related in the well-known Algonkian myth.[3]

As all the references to the origin of the Sauk bundles that occur in earlier literature corroborate the statements that the bundles originated with Wi'sakä, the writer is forced to the conclusion that Mr. Harrington's data relate, not to the origin of all the bundles in the tribe, but to the personal experiences of some individual bundle owner, perhaps a member of the Wolf gens. In this connection it is significant that the Prairie Potawatomi at one time attributed the origin of their bundles, especially those for war, to Wi'sakä.

Mr. Harrington himself quotes an account by the Rev. Cutting Marsh[4] which was furnished him by the writer, and in which the origin of the sacred bundles is traced through Wi'sakä.[5]

A still better and fuller account, paralleling the statements of the Rev. Marsh, is to be found in Galland's writings.[6] As these articles are rather difficult of access to most students, the writer will paraphrase or quote the greater portion of the parts dealing with the origin myth of the sacred bundles.

In the beginning, after the creation, the universe was inhabited by vast numbers of supernatural beings, prominent among whom were the Ai-yam-woy (Aiyûmowä, plural—wûk) or giants, the Mah-she-ken-a-pek (Mishîkine'bîk) or great horned serpent, and the Nah-me-pa-she (namipêshi) or underneath panther. These monsters were placed by the Great Spirit in the sea, while Wi'sakä the culture hero, was put on the land to govern it, and to him was also given control over the powers of the water. Mankind were made in the likeness of Wi'sakä and placed on this island, the earth, and given the knowledge of fire, since they were devoid of fur or feathers.

In course of time the giant Aiyamwoy overran both earth and sea, and threatened mankind with extinction. At this juncture, according to Marsh, Wi'sakä sent his brother Nah-pat-tay to the gods of the sea to remonstrate, whereupon they slew him. In the Galland version the underworld powers prepared a feast to which they invited

[3]Skinner, Alanson, "Folklore of the Menomini Indians," Am. Mus. Nat. Hist., Anthropological Papers, Vol. XIII, Pt. 3, N. Y., 1918.
Jones, William, "Fox Texts," Publ. Am. Ethnological Soc., Vol. I, Leyden, 1907.

[4]Marsh, Rev. Cutting, "Documents Relating to the Stockbridge Mission," 1825-48, Wis. Hist. Coll. Vol. XV, pp. 129-138, 1900.

[5]In a letter to the writer dated February 18th, 1923, Mr. Harrington says: "I am sure you are right about the origin of the Mishâman. The tales I collected are doubtless the origins of individual bundles to which the tellers attributed a greater importance than they deserved."

[6]Galland, Dr. Isaac, "The Indian Tribes of the West" The Annals of Iowa, Vol. VII, No. 4, p. 350 et seq.

Wi'sakä in order to slay him, but were frustrated by his brother, whom they discovered among them, and whom they killed in his place.

Wi'sakä mourned for his brother for ten days, which accounts for the fasting of the Sauk in modern times. The gods sent back his dead brother after the tenth day, but Wi'sakä refused to receive him, and sent him on to the other world to rule the souls of the dead. Thus death came to mankind, and resurrection of the body was prohibited.

Wi'sakä then destroyed the Aiyamwoy with fire, and was attacked by the other netherworld powers with the aid of Papoan-a-tes-sa, the God of the North, who tried to freeze Wi'sakä, but failed.

Next they caused a flood, but Wi'sakä and certain animals and men escaped by means of a raft or a bubble which floated on the surface. When the storms were over, Wi'sakä caused the tortoise and then the muskrat to dive for earth. The muskrat, although drowned in the attempt, yet clutched earth in its paws, so that with this as a nucleus, Wi'sakä built another world.

Wi'sakä then divided the ancestors of the Sauk into two groups, one called O-ke-mau-uk, or chieftains, the other Us-kaup-a, servants, or Mam-ish-aum-uk, Cooks, or Bundle Keepers (?).[7] The first division he divided into the following six gentes:

1. Pau-kau-hau-moi	4. Great Sea
2. Sturgeon	5. Bear
3. Eagle	6. Thunder

The second group was divided as follows:

1. Water	4. Turkey
2. Deer	5. Wolf
3. Bear-potato	6. Fox

The priests and attendants for ceremonies were to be chosen only from the latter group. (Probably this is a reference to the division of the gentes for reciprocal ceremonial functions, rather than a division of the tribe into moieties.)

According to Marsh, at this time Wi'sakä gave a mîshâm to the head of each family, in which the story of the world's origin is recorded in songs. Later, Wi'sakä, forgetting that he was a creature of the Great Spirit, boasted that he had himself driven the evil spirits from the world, but the Great Spirit opened his own sacred bundle and showed Wi'sakä his origin. This shamed Wi'sakä, who fasted ten

---

[7]The writer suspects that this should be Māmishiwûk, Attendants.

days in expiation, but the Great Spirit banished him to the end of the earth and placed the God of Winter between him and mankind.

The Galland version is fuller, and says that after the rehabilitation of mankind, Wi'sakä ordered them to give sacrifices and feasts in his memory and to the Great Spirit, specifying that they must sing the sacred song of the gens to which the master of ceremonies upon that occasion, belonged. He further gave minute instructions as to how to give feasts.

"After this manner ye shall make sacrifice to Monato-kush-a, and observe a feast in the memory of Wis-uk-a, through all your generations hereafter. When any one belonging to your tribe shall determine to observe this sacred ordinance, after providing a clean animal for his feast, he shall first send forth from his wik-e-aup (i. e., house or lodge,) his women and children; he shall then call a few of his own clan to the feast, and when these shall have come into the lodge, and the mam-ish-aum-uk having returned, he shall command him to kill the victim which he has provided for the sacrifice, and also to cook, prepare, and arrange the feast.

"Then he shall bring forth his mish-aum, and shall open it in the presence of his companions. The mam-ish-aum-uk shall then bring into the lodge the victim slain for the sacrifice, and lay it before the mish-aum, and shall take some incense (tobacco) from the mish-aum, and dividing it into five parcels, he shall tie to each leg a parcel, and one parcel to the neck of the victim, and being appropriately painted, it shall remain before the feast fire until the close of the feast.

"The master of the feast shall then take some incense from the mish-aum and cast it into the fire to make a sweet, savory perfume unto Monato-kush-a. He shall also make two holes in the earth, one at each end of the feast fire, and into these holes he shall cast tobacco and fire to make the earth smoke. And, having done this, he shall speak to Monato-kusk-a thus:

" 'O, thou who hast made all things, both upon the earth and in the sea, it is unto thee that I have fasted and cried; the trees of the forest have witnessed my sorrow and affliction; and I trust that the mountain's echo has borne my supplications to thine ears. This feast which I have prepared is in memory of thee and Wis-uk-a; accept therefore in this victim, my best beast, the animal most admired by me, and the especial favorite of my family. In offering it unto thee in sacrifice, I follow the ordinance of Wis-uk-a. Grant me this favor, that I may live long upon the earth. Make me strong in

the day of battle, and cause the terror of my face to spread confusion
in the ranks, and dismay and trembling through the hearts of my
enemies.

" 'Give me, in dreams, a true and faithful warning of every approaching danger, and guard me against the evils to come.'

"Then the master of the feast shall commence the feast song, and
shall invite his companions to join him in singing the sacred song of
his clan, and they shall continue to sing until the meat provided for
the feast is thoroughly cooked. He shall then send for all whom he
chooses to come to his feast; and when they shall have come into the
lodge the us-kaup shall divide the whole of the festive animal into
equal portions, according to the number of invited guests, who shall
always bring with them to feast each man his own dish, in which the
us-kaup shall serve the meat; and he shall direct the us-kaup to place
the whole head of the festive animal upon the dish of that man whom
he desires to honor, and whom he esteems as the most valiant among
his guests. When every man's dish, with his portion thereon, has been
set before him, and sufficient time has been given for the food to cool,
the master of the feast shall give a signal to the guests to commence
eating; each man shall then devour his portion in the shortest time
possible; meanwhile the master of the feast and his companions shall
resume and continue to sing their sacred song, until the guests have
consumed the food. And when they have finished eating, the us-kaup
shall collect all the bones and cast them into the fire, or a stream of
running water, that the dogs defile them not.

"The feast now being ended, some one of the guests shall now
address the assembly thus:

" 'To all who are here assembled to participate in the commemoration of Wis-uk-a, around this sacred food—know ye, that it
is the good will and pleasure of Wis-uk-a that we should in this manner
celebrate his memory and observe his holy ordinance. Our worthy
entertainer, in whose lodge we have just now feasted, and who is
our brother, has opened in our presence his most holy mish-aum, and
he and his companions have sung in our ears the delightful sacred song
of his forefathers, which has been handed down from generation to
generation, since the days of Wis-uk-a, to our present respected
brother.

" 'In this most holy mish-aum are not only the symbols of all
our sacred songs, but it also contains all the necessary rules for the
Government of our lives and the regulation of our conduct.   Our

duties to Monato-kush-a, and to each other, are herein represented by signs prepared by Wis-uk-a himself, and which have been collected from the purest and most wonderful portions of the whole creation. Remember, therefore, to teach your children faithfully to observe all things which are taught by the sacred symbols of this holy mish-aum, that Monato-kush-a may look on us with pleasure, and prosper our journey in the path of life.' "

"The mam-ish-aum-uk shall then take up the sacrifice victim from before the Mish-aum and carry it forth from the lodge to some convenient place beyond the limits of the town or encampment, accompanied by all the assembly; there they shall hang it up, by the neck, upon a tree or pole, painted red with red clay, its face looking towards the east. The ordinance of the feast and sacrifice being in this manner observed and accomplished, every man shall return to his own lodge."

"Then Wis-uk-a called the band of O-ke-mau-uk-a, and delivered to the head man of each clan the holy mish-aum and charged them as follows:

"WIS-UK-A'S CHARGE TO THE O-KE-MAU-UK-A

" 'Keep this in memory of grey antiquity. This holy depository contains the symbolic memorials of Wis-uk-a, his history of the earth, and his commands to the human race. In this sacred repository ye shall find the signs which represent all your duties to Monato-kush-a, your obligations to each other, and a confident promise, which will assure you of prosperity in this life, and happiness and glory beyond the dark forest of that river which ye must cross soon after death. If ye will have a due respect to the teachings of these sacred symbols, and strictly observe the sacred ordinances, and do them, then ye shall retain the vigor of youth even to old age, ye shall increase in the land, and your multitudes shall cover the whole earth. Ye shall eat the fat beasts of the forests, the fish of the waters and the fowls of the air; and ye shall be clothed in warm garments of wool and fur skins. Your young men shall return victorious from battle; your young women shall come in at evening loaded with the rich fruits of the earth; and at night young children shall rejoice in the dance. Ye shall be clothed with strength all the days of your lives; your faces shall be a terror to your enemies, and in battle they shall not be able to stand before you. Your lives shall be prolonged upon the earth;

and when ye die, you shall pass joyfully over that horrid mountain and awful river which separates this earth from the spirit home. And ye shall be in no danger of falling into that gloomy gulf where the wicked and disobedient are punished; but with rejoicing ye shall join your ancestors (who observed the ordinances) in that happy land where pleasures and glory are prepared for you, of which you can now form no correct estimate, and where sorrows and afflictions never shall come.' ''

At the conclusion of this harangue, Wi′sakä opened the misham and took out the various articles contained therein, and explained them as rules for the guidance of mankind. The rules given by Galland are six in number, and are:

1. Youths are required to fast each day of winter for twenty winters.
2. Young men are required to fast for a vision when twenty years old.
3. Women are required to be secluded during menstruation.
4. Women are required to undergo purification after parturition.
5. Children are to be named at a ceremony held six months after birth.
6. Lying is forbidden.

To these the Rev. Marsh adds the following:

7. To fast when vengeance is desired upon the enemy.
8. To hold a ceremony whenever a bear or other large game is killed.
9. To be generous to the poor.

These evidently correspond to the rules of life said to be part of the teachings of the Medicine Lodge Society.

It is very evident that the rites and myths of the origin of the sacred bundles form only a part of the great Culture Hero Cycle of the Central Algonkian people, which is the fundamental sacred myth of the entire area, and especially connected with the myth of origin of the medicine lodge. The importance of this cycle and the part which the Culture Hero plays in the life of the Central Algonkians cannot be overemphasized.[8]

That present day Indians ascribe the origin of the sacred bundles to Wi′sakä through the deception of Turtle, is probably but a recent

[8]Skinner, Alanson. "Social Life and Ceremonial Bundles of the Menomini Indians," Am. Mus. Nat. Hist., Anthropological Papers, Vol. XII, pp. 1-165.

Skinner, Alanson. "Observations on the Ethnology of the Sauk Indians," Bull. Milw. Pub. Mus., Vol. V, pp. 1-57.

degeneration of old ideas. Sauk life and beliefs have disintegrated so much in the past century through their ignorance of the true beliefs of their ancestors, that the garbling of what they do know is not at all remarkable. Another generation of the Sauk will likely be wholly ignorant of the mythology of their forefathers.

THE CULTURE HERO MYTH

With the above facts in mind, it is plain that there can be no doubt but that the Culture Hero Cycle is the great fundamental religious myth of the Central and Northern Algonkians, perhaps of all the Woodland members of the stock. In its pristine form it consisted of the following parts:

1. The creation of the earth by the Great Spirit (The Sun).
2. The personification of the earth in the Earth Mother.
3. The magic birth of her daughter.
4. The virgin birth of the Culture Hero as a child of the primal forces.
5. The destruction of evil powers and the obtaining of benefits for the races of men by the Culture Hero, including for example the theft of fire and the capture of tobacco.
6. The murder of the Culture Hero's brother by the Gods of the Nether World.
7. The wounding of the principal Nether World Gods by the Hero.
8. The killing of the Nether World Gods by the Hero disguised as a doctor.
9. The deluge sent in revenge by the surviving Powers Below.
10. The escape of the Hero and the recreation of the world with earth brought up by the diving animals.
11. The return of the slain brother of the hero, who is refused by him and sent to govern the Realm of the Dead. (The prohibition of resurrection of the body.)
12. The council of the Powers Below with Those Above resulting in the offering of the rites of the Medicine Lodge to the Hero.
13. The initiation of the Hero into the Medicine Lodge. (Thus securing long life on earth and resurrection of the spirit.)
14. The Hero obtains the sacred bundles for mankind, assuring success in war and the chase.

15. Having taught mankind how to live, and prepared the earth
for them, the Culture Hero withdraws to the north, where
he now remains.

To this heroic epic have been added a series of coarse and vulgar
tales originally part of a trickster cycle concerning the Great Hare, an
animal that figures widely as a buffoon in other areas. This has happened largely by the degeneration, through word of mouth, of the
original name of the Culture Hero, the Great Dawn, into the Great
Rabbit or Hare, because these two names are extremely similar in
many Algonkian dialects, for example, in Menomini, Mätc Wapan
means Great Dawn, or Light, whereas Mätc Wapus means Great
Hare, which is now given as the correct form for Mä"näbus (or Mä"-
näpus) the name of the Culture Hero.

This seems the more probable because the Eastern Dakota, the
Ioway, Oto, and Winnebago, who were in close contact with the
Central Algonkians, and whose culture has been most strongly in-
fluenced by them, but who do not have such similar terms for the
Culture Hero and the Trickster, still possess both cycles as separate
series.

At the present time no Algonkian tribe of the region under dis-
cussion is known to have the great Culture Hero epic in its entirety.
The long and determined destructive teachings of the missionaries
have so broken down and confused the original traditions that we
are obliged to glean remnants here and there and thus piece together
the whole.   For example, probably the best recorded version of the
segments concerning the origin of the Medicine Lodge is that of the
Menomini[9] who also present the best account of the origin of certain
portable shrines, the sacred hunting bundles. On the other hand, the
beginning of the still more important war bundles is best derived from
the Sauk, as has just been demonstrated.   The latter also give a better
general account of the teachings of the Culture Hero with regard to
other matters than can at present be found in print, although the
writer has heard many similar statements made by the Menomini
during his residence among them.

That Harrington found that some of the Sauk attributed the
origin of their war bundles to Pitoskah' and the writer that the Menomini supposed theirs came from Wata'kwûna, another hero, is no
doubt due to the habit of the modern Indians in associating the names

---

[9]Skinner, Alanson, "Medicine Ceremony of the Menomini, Iowa, and Wahpeton Indians," Mus.
Amer. Indian, Heye Foundation, Indian Notes and Monographs, Vol. IV.

of famous individuals with certain particular bundles, and hence eventually attributing the origin of all bundles of that type to the personal adventures of these persons. What makes this more probable is that Harrington in his brief study of the Ioway heard from even as well informed an Indian as the late Chief David Tohee that all their war bundles were obtained by a man named Wanethû'ng'ê. But the writer, in the course of his more protracted work discovered that this Wanethû'ng'ê was a person who lived but a generation ago, who was indeed, the uncle of one of his informants.

But, Wanethû'ng'ê was a person of most extraordinary super-natural powers. He was known not only to the Ioway and their immediate neighbors, but even to the Eastern Dakota, several of whom were acquainted with him, as the writer has learned through his Wahpeton friends. Wanethû'ng'ê had a very famous bundle, which Mr. Harrington was fortunately able to secure for the Museum of the American Indian, Heye Foundation, but the bundle itself, from the mere evidence of its contents, must far antedate the period of Wanethû'ng'ê's life, since even in his time scarcely more than a generation ago, porcupine quillwork, for example, was a thing of the past among the Ioway. The truth of the matter is that the Ioway have a real origin myth concerning the provenience of the sacred bundles which has nothing whatever to do with Wanethû'ng'ê, and which was already hoary with antiquity when he was born. In the story of Dore and Wahredua we are told that these heroes, the familiar "Lodge Boy and Throw Away" of the Plains, secured all the known types of bundles successively from the gods of the four corners of the universe.

Thus we have abundant proof that the Marsh and Galland versions of the origin of the war bundles of the Sauk through the Culture Hero, backed as they are by the Menomini hunting bundle myths[10], are substantially correct, even if not now known to the natives.

In other words, the real traditional origin of the sacred bundles of the Central Algonkians goes back to the great fundamental epic of the Culture Hero Cycle, upon which all their ancient religious beliefs and rites, and, as mentioned before, perhaps those of all the Woodland Algonkians[11] are founded.

---

[10]Skinner, Alanson, "Social Life and Ceremonial Bundles of Menomini Indians," Am. Mus. Nat. Hist., Anthropological Papers, Vol. XII, Part I, pp. 1-165.

[11]Brinton, "Myths of the New World," pp. 194 et seq. (note footnote p. 200, for reference to belief of Virginia Algonkian), Phila., 1905.

OBSERVATIONS ON THE USE AND CARE
OF WAR BUNDLES

When a war bundle is to be taken from its repository to another lodge on the occasion of a feast or other ceremony, it must be re-wrapped and tied. This also requires a feast for the purpose. Again, after having been used in a successful campaign, especially if a portion of a scalp is placed inside, the roots and herb medicines contained in any bundle, and the tobacco sacrifices therein, must be renewed. In any event the medicinal part of the contents should be renewed every three to five years. A new reed whistle is added to the outside of a bundle after each return from a successful war party. When the bundle is opened at the next buffalo dance the leader uses the new whistle.

All sacred bundles should be opened at least four times a year at the Spring feast, Roasting Ear feast, Autumn feast, given when the leaves fall, and Winter feast, about the first of January.

Most bundles are merely opened and their contents exposed as they lie upon the deerskin wrapper, but the Bear-potato Gens war bundle receives somewhat different treatment. The two scalp trimmed otters are taken and placed with their heads towards the fire, and slightly raised, the bundle of sticks which forms the rack upon which they are supported when in use, being laid under their necks.

At a Bear-potato Gens war bundle feast the waiter keeps the head, brisket, and feet of the dog that is eaten, and calls his own particular friends of the Bear and Fish gentes, which furnish the waiters for Bear-potato ceremonies, to eat with him.

Ordinarily Sauk war bundles are treated with the greatest consideration. They are kept sacredly, away from all intruders, especially from women who may be menstruating, and are carried and handled only when necessary, and then with the greatest reverence. Tobacco sacrifices are made to them at intervals, and the feasts are religiously given for them. On the other hand, Mê'siwûk once knew a warrior who, before going into battle, always used to throw his bundle on the ground with all his force, and thus "infuriate it so that it would fight the better for him." When the bundle was thus enraged, he would demand of it the life of the bravest man among the enemy.

PRESENT STATUS OF THE BELIEF IN THE EFFICACY OF WAR BUNDLES

At the present writing the Sauk have all but abandoned their belief in the efficacy of the sacred bundles. Few, if any, know the rituals entire, but many regard them with superstitious awe, even though they may not keep up the feasts or use the shrines themselves. This is true of Indians who have abandoned the native mode of living and who follow the customs of the peyote eaters or of the various Christian sects. Many an Indian who has sacred bundles hanging in his bark house or the loft of his barn will allow them to fall to pieces rather than care for them, yet will not sell them to an alien lest their disposal bring on "the end of the world."

The more conservative Menomini in the forests of northern Wisconsin still regard the bundles with much of the same awe as in olden times. A letter from the writer's Menomini Uncle by adoption lies before him, and reads in part:

"Änä'mekût Osake'wûk! Änäma'wûk! The Dog-like Sauk! All dogs! Our ancestor's bundles conquered them so that they (fled and) left their breech cloths too soon, as our old war song has repeated until it went to dust!"

The passage of nearly a hundred years has neither erased the memory of Sauk raids from the minds of the Menomini nor softened their rancor towards their ancient enemies, for when the writer told his Menomini relatives that he had been among the Sauk lodges in Oklahoma, they asked if he had seen any of the scalps of their women and children there. When he told them that he had obtained Sauk bundles for the Museum, they replied in scorn that he had doubtless bought them cheap, since they had no power anyway!

CONTENTS OF THE SACRED WAR BUNDLES

In Mr. Harrington's admirable study of the "Sacred Bundles of the Sac and Fox Indians" so often referred to in this paper, he lists and describes the contents of twenty-two Sauk bundles obtained by his efforts in Oklahoma. Inasmuch as the work has been well and painstakingly done, no attempt will be made to go into full details in this paper, and the writer will confine himself to figuring and describing that material obtained for the Public Museum of the City of Milwaukee which differs from or supplements that collected by Mr. Harrington.

In theory, at least, the bundles are supposed to differ in contents according to gens. Mr. Harrington does not record the gentes represented by the bundles which he obtained, although those collected from the late Mêshê'bêkwa are undoubtedly of the Wolf gens and those from the late Cokwiwa of the Bear-potato gens. Mr. Harrington gives a partial tabulation of the commoner articles in the bundles which he gathered, and we find that of the twenty-two that he describes, twenty held parts of the buffalo, eighteen eagle feathers, eighteen birdskin amulets, fourteen fawnskin wrappers or amulets, and twelve amulets of swan's down.

The commoner articles in the bundles obtained by the writer, are listed in the tabulation on the following page.

Unfortunately no Fox bundles are at hand for comparison. Two from Tama, Iowa, in the possession of the Field Museum of Natural History at Chicago, examined by the writer some time ago, agreed remarkably in appearance and general contents with those of the Sauk. Both, it is interesting to observe, contained tanned deerskin breech clouts or war kilts, with some slight porcupine quill ornamentation.

Dr. Truman Michelson of the Smithsonian Institution of Washington, D. C., has written a very interesting paper entitled "The Owl Sacred Pack of the Fox Indians."[12] As the bundle seems to be most unusual in contents, judging by the bundles of the Sauk and the two Fox bundles in the Field Museum, and, as the vendor of the bundle and informant as to its rites, the late Alfred Kiyana, was of very dubious reputation, the writer hesitates to use the material for comparison.

The general outward appearance of the sacred bundles of the Sauk is quite well known, and no one can spend any length of time among this tribe without becoming familiar with them. They are oblong packages wrapped in smoke-blackened and crackled deerskin, bound with leathern thongs, with reed whistles, gourd rattles, and, occasionally, war clubs, lashed to the outside. They usually hang in groups in the gens ceremonial bark house and strangers are not allowed to approach and examine them too closely. In plate II, fig. 2, may be seen an ordinary war bundle of the Wolf gens, and in fig. 1 of the same plate the charging bundle of the same gens, elsewhere described.

[12]Bur. of Am. Ethnology, Bull. 72, Washington, 1921.

ANALYSES OF 25 WAR BUNDLES

General Characteristics: All have one or more tanned deerskin wrappers. All have one or more cane whistles attached.

No. of Bdls.	Gentes	Objects of Buffalo skin or hair	Eagle plumes or shafts	Prisoner Ties	Objects of Otter fur	Weasel skin amulets	Bird skin amulets	Fawn skin amulets	Swan's down amulets	Yarn and bead amulets
10	Wolf	51	2	1	0	0	8	13	9	3
5	Turkey	0	9	3	2	1	15	6	11	1
4	Bear-potato	10	1	1	2	0	4	5	3	0
1	Elk	3	0	0	0	1	1	3	1	1
2	Beaver	1	0	1	3	0	2	0	0	0
2	Buffalo	14	1	0	0	0	0	1	3	3
1	Deer	0	0	0	0	0	1	0	0	0
25		79	13	6	7	2	31	28	27	8

Two bundles, one from the Fish and one from the Bear clan, have been examined by the writer since the above tabulation was made. Both were badly mixed together, but apparently contained articles of buffalo fur, fawn skin, swan's down and otter fur.

In plate III, fig. 1, is shown a war belt from a bundle of the Bear-potato gens. It consists of a girdle of tanned buckskin, handsomely embroidered with porcupine quills in scarlet, black, yellow, and white. At the rear depends an ornament made of raven feathers, to some of which deer's hair dyed scarlet and tabs of weasel skin are attached. The central part of the ornament, however, is a wolf's tail, from which depend quilled ornaments and metallic jinglers. It is an unusually fine specimen, although not equal to that figured and described by Harrington[13]. Native opinions differ as to whether it was worn by the partizan before and during battle, or given to the first warrior to count a coup to wear during the ceremonial return of the war party, and the subsequent dancing.

There is no difference of opinion among the Indians about the use of the eagle plumes with quilled shaft ornaments shown in plate III, figs. 2-5. These were awarded to the first four warriors of the Turkey gens to perform deeds of valor in any action in which the bundle that contained them was used. They were worn on the return of the party and were emblems of their exploits. Three of the four feathers are dyed red, and this is said to signify that the wearers actually killed and scalped foemen with their own hands. The white or natural feather merely represents some other form of valor.

In plate IV are shown the stuffed skins of two otters, adorned with wisps of hair and fragments of human scalps. These have been described in some detail elsewhere in this paper. In plate V are shown two similar articles, fig. 1 being the skin of an adult beaver to which are fastened fragments and wisps of no less than forty separate human scalps. One eye is missing, but the other is formed by a bone or shell disk bead of ancient type, the material being difficult of determination. The use of this remarkable object by the warriors and partizans of the Beaver gens, to which the bundle belonged, was no doubt similar to that ascribed to the scalp otters of the Bear-potato gens. The war bundle which held this specimen contained practically nothing else, with the exception of numerous tobacco offerings. It is of interest to note that a number of the scalps, especially those attached to the nose or mouth, are of light brown hair and are probably those of white-men.

Fig. 2, plate V, shows the skin of an animal resembling, but not certainly, an otter, which was the chief contents of another Beaver

---

[13]Ibid, p. 197, plate XXVII. Also in "A Bird-quill Belt of the Sauk and Fox Indians." Mus. Am. Indian, Heye Foundation, Notes and Monographs, Vol. X, No. 5, N. Y., 1920.

gens bundle. It has three wisps of human hair, not properly scalps, but so considered by the Sauk, attached to its mouth. Its legs are ornamented with spirally wrapped narrow woven bands of scarlet, yellow, and black porcupine quillwork in alternate bands.

In plate VI are shown two deerskin war kilts from different war bundles of the Turkey gens. The first, fig. 1, is rather plain, but has an upper border folded over and embroidered on the edge with a line of brightly colored porcupine quills in yellow, black, and scarlet, and some pendant metallic jinglers with quill-wrapped fringe. There are three short horizontal lines of scarlet quills, and a row of metallic jinglers filled with scarlet deer's hair along the bottom.

Fig. 2 of the same plate, shows a more highly ornamental war kilt. Quilled deerskin thongs with metallic jinglers are attached at intervals along the upper border, and from the center depends a quilled thong pendant terminating in a tuft of hair from a buffalo tail. The quillwork is in the usual yellow, scarlet and black. Three crosses in yellow and red quillwork appear on the face of the kilt, and the bottom is fringed with metal jinglers. The corners, as in the preceding specimen, are elongated, and, in this instance, there occur tufts of raven feathers, quilled at the base, the point of attachment.

These kilts are said to have been worn by successful partizans of the Turkey gens on the return of the victorious war party.

In plate VII, fig. 1, is a headdress made of a split raven skin, worn with the head over the owner's forehead. It is from a war bundle of the Beaver gens, which contained two of these headdresses. These are the only examples of raven skin which the writer has noted, although hawk skin headdresses are frequent.

Figs. 2 and 4 of the same plate, represent hawkskin headdresses of the same type as the raven above mentioned. The first example comes from a war bundle of the Bear-potato gens. The ornamental strips on the wings with porcupine quill decoration in black, yellow, and scarlet, are well preserved. In fig. 4, a hawkskin hat from a bundle of the Wolf gens exhibits the same phenomenon of the handsomely quilled wing strips.

Fig. 3, plate VII, displays a very remarkable buffalo horn headdress, also from a war bundle of the Wolf gens. To a foundation of deerskin and red blanketing have been added two buffalo horns, or perhaps, portions of the same horn split and shaved thin. The crown of the headdress has been covered with bunches of deer or antelope hair attached with sinew, but the most unusual feature is the band of blue and white cylindrical glass beads, imitation wampum, which crosses the crown. It is woven on the style of a wampum belt or short band, on blanket ravellings twisted into yarn. Such examples are very rare, even in the collections of the largest museums, there being on record far more examples of actual wampum than of the imitation article.

Plate VII, fig. 5, shows one of the most remarkable specimens from the Sauk in the Public Museum of the City of Milwaukee. It is a war kilt made of a long broad belt of red blanketing to which is attached a fringe of cut rawhide carefully wrapped with porcupine quills in dingy yellow, with some irregular square figures in rusty brown, now faded almost beyond recognition. A little more than midway to the bottom are attached many dew claws of the deer, probably the forerunners of the metal jinglers so often seen on later specimens. The specimen seems to be very old and no doubt antedates the red cloth belt to which it is attached. The dyes are obviously native, and the quillwork itself resembles much of the old work on the dance and society paraphernalia of the Arapaho. It comes from a bundle of the Buffalo gens.

In plate VIII, figs. 1-3, are shown three buffalo tail amulets, figs.1 and 3 being head ornaments, and fig. 2 an arm band ornamented with porcupine quill decoration. The designs in fig. 1 are done in red, yellow, and green; in fig. 2 in red and yellow with small black specks; and in fig. 3 in red, yellow, black, blue, green, and white. All are amulets worn into battle by the warriors of the Wolf gens (figs. 1 and 2), and the Bear-potato gens (fig. 3) in order to give them the power and ferocity of the angry buffalo.

In fig. 4, plate VIII, is shown a shoulder throw or garter made of netted thongs wrapped in porcupine quills dyed crimson, with a central figure of hourglass shape in yellow and black concentric lines. The very long fringe is completely wrapped with quills in crimson, yellow, and black, except the extreme tips. To the specimen are tied numerous small packets of medicine wrapped in buckskin, and an antique small or toy razor with tortoise shell handles. It may be a war belt, but information was not to be had of the natives as to its use, as the owner of the bundle from which it was taken had long been dead. It was a shrine of the Turkey gens.

In plate IX, figs. 1 and 3, are shown two ties for prisoners taken from war bundles of the Bear-potato and Wolf gentes, respectively. They are made of braided Indian hemp fibre with pendants ornamented with red and yellow porcupine quillwork in the case of fig. 3, and with a number of strands of braided human hair in the case of fig. 1.

Fig. 2 of the same plate represents a prisoner tie from a war bundle of the Beaver gens that is braided from yarn made of the undyed wool of the buffalo.

Fig. 4, plate IX, represents a buffalo tail amulet to be worn on the rear of a warrior's belt while in combat. It is adorned with the scalp of an Ivory-billed woodpecker, and some thong bangles quilled in red and yellow. It is from a war bundle of the Bear-potato gens.

The buffalo tail and swan's down head ornament or amulet shown in fig. 5 of the same plate, is from a war bundle of the Wolf gens. It is decorated with several long thongs of buckskin wound at intervals with faded yellow porcupine quills, the effect being somewhat like strung beads.

Fig. 6 of plate IX, represents a small medicine pouch, similar to those of beadwork found in sacred bundles and medicine bags among all the central western tribes. It is, however, made of a netted thongwork, the thongs being wrapped with crimson quills, with a border design and diamonds in yellow. It was obtained in a medicine bag made from the skin of an animal resembling an albino raccoon. Fig. 8 on the same plate is an antique example of the same type of pouch made of old time "pony-trader" beads, the coarse beads, which tradition says were one of the early varieties packed in to the Indian settlements of the interior on horseback by adventurous white traders. The colors are white and blue, and it was found in a war bundle of the Wolf gens.

Fig. 7, plate IX, is a buffalo tail head amulet with a pennant of red blanketing upon which is embroidered the conventional outline of a thunderbird in yellow quillwork, with lightning symbols beneath in the same material and color. It comes from a war bundle of the Bear-potato gens.

Plate IX, fig. 9 shows a buffalo tail amulet wrapped in a band of woven yarn mingled with coarse white "pony trader" beads. The yarn is mottled with reddish and yellow dyes. It is from a war bundle of the Wolf gens.

In plate X, fig. 1, is represented a warrior's personal charm necklace made of braided sweet grass with ornaments of twisted strips of otter fur. It is not from a war bundle, and was the property of an old Sauk Indian named Jesse James.

The extraordinary medicine pouch shown in plate X, fig. 2, is made from the skin of one of the legs of an albino buffalo. It is ornamented with thongs quilled in red and yellow, and metallic jinglers containing hair dyed scarlet. It held, among other objects, a small metal box supposed to contain portions of the dried tongues of infants, slain by magic by the owner of the bundle, who, it was said, was able to use his bundle for witchcraft as well as war, an unusual state of affairs. It was obtained from a member of the Wolf gens.

A part of the contents of a war bundle obtained in the Wolf gens bundle house of the Sauk, but said to have been the property of the Wolf gens of the related Kickapoo, is worthy of consideration in this section of this paper. When the writer saw this bundle hanging in the Sauk ceremonial house, and attempted to purchase it from the then bundle keeper of the Wolf gens, the late Austen Grant, son of the late Mêshê'bêkwa, he was told that it was not the property of any Sauk. Years ago, Grant said, a Kickapoo war party, on their way home from a raid, presumably on some other tribe of Oklahoma or Indian Territory, came to the members of their own clan among the Sauk, and explained that as they had taken four scalps, they were afraid of Government punishment, and begged permission to hang their war bundle with the Wolf clan bundles of the Sauk until the trouble blew over. This the Sauk permitted, but the Kickapoo had never dared to reclaim it.

The writer's Sauk interpreter, the Reverend Wm. Harris, later went to the Kickapoo near McCloud, Oklahoma, and succeeded in finding the sole surviving relative of one of the men of the war party, a woman, who claimed the right to the bundle. He purchased it of her, went to the Wolf gens house of the Sauk himself, took down the bundle, and forwarded it to Milwaukee. It is of interest as being the only authentic war bundle of the Kickapoo which has ever passed out of the keeping of the tribe, so far as the writer's knowledge extends.

It does not contain the four scalps ascribed to it by Sauk tradition, but there are therein a number of imitation scalps of buffalo skin and hair. It has the usual deerskin wrappers, reed whistles, and other paraphernalia found in Sauk bundles. Worthy of especial mention, however, are the articles shown in plate XI.

Fig. 1, plate XI, is an antler spatula, designed for the mixing of medicines. Fig. 2 is an amulet made of weasel skin in the white winter coat, to the nose of which are attached two rattlesnake rattles and a wisp of a human scalp. Fig. 3 shows a very fine antique prisoner tie of Indian hemp made with a broad woven band to pass around the neck of the captive, like an Iroquois burden strap, and with false embroidery in dyed deer hair. The colors are the usual crimson, yellow, black and faded blue or green. The design, which is not very well brought out in the plate, because of the difficulty in obtaining the full color values, is divided into two bilaterally unsymmetrical zones, reminding one of the lack of symmetry in the decorated flaps of Sauk, Fox, and Prairie Potawatomi moccasins. The portion to the left has a crimson background, with three yellow lines at the end, and a geometrical figure in black with a yellow border in the center. The middle of the design area is cut by several closely set vertical lines, and then come three groups of oblique linked rectangles in several colors, while the right end is finished off with another group of three vertical lines. There are metallic jinglers and the usual quilled fringe on this fine specimen.

Fig. 4, plate XI, shows an ordinary prisoner tie of braided Indian hemp fibre with quilled attachments in red and yellow, and metal jinglers.

NOTES ON WEAPONS

In plate XII, figs. 1 and 3, are shown several ancient flint tipped arrows which, with some pointed headless arrows, and the original bow, are said to have been brought from Wisconsin by the Sauk ancestors of Mêshê'bêkwa who kept them as heirlooms. The bow itself is said to have seen service against the whites in the Black Hawk War, now nearly a century ago. The points are of dull grayish flint, and of a common coarse notched Wisconsin type. The bow is a plain notched stave with twisted sinew string. The paintings on the arrow shafts are reminiscent of those on some old antler and bone tipped arrows from the east in the Peabody Museum of Harvard University at Cambridge, Mass. These latter are figured and described by Willoughby in the American Anthropologist.[14] The third arrow, fig. 2, of the same plate, was obtained from a brother of the vendor of the others at a different locality, but is likely one of the same set, although the Sauk owner was ignorant of its history.

War clubs, both of the flat and ball headed variety, were in use by the Sauk, and while one of the former was seen attached to a war bundle of the Fish clan, it could not be obtained. A very fine example of the ball headed variety is in the American Museum of Natural

---

[14]Willoughby, C. C., "Antler-pointed Arrows of the Southeastern Indians," Am. Anthropologist, N. S. Vol. 3, p. 431, 1901.

History at New York, and is said to have been captured by a white soldier during the Black Hawk War. War clubs of any kind are now very rare among the Sauk.

In spite of the pictures made by Catlin of the Sauk met by him during the early part of the nineteenth century, many of which show them carrying buffalo hide shields, the Indians of today deny that they ever used shields. Of course it is possible that the custom has died out and left no recollection among the people.

War spears or lances, called tcima'gûn, were used extensively, but cannot now be found. They had cedar shafts about seven feet long, it is said, which were covered with red list cloth, to which eagle feathers and beaded ornaments were attached, while scalps were fastened near the point or blade. Some examples are said to have been fourteen feet in length, but these had plain uncovered handles. Few of the Woodland Indians used lances, but to this rule the Sauk, Fox, Prairie Potawatomi, and perhaps the Kickapoo, were exceptions.

MISCELLANEOUS

From Jesse James, a Sauk Indian residing near Avery, Oklahoma, was obtained a personal war medicine (sagasu), or "preventative." It consists of a small woven yarn bag in which are a number of small packets of medicine, which are taken, chewed, and sprayed over the body to render the user invulnerable. A small box, made of metal, and no doubt an old fashioned snuff box, is lined with white down, and contains merely some small pieces of white earth. The down is said to symbolize the earth, and the pieces of clay the sky or heaven.

This, with the exception of the sweet grass and otter fur necklace obtained from the same individual, and shown in plate X, fig. 1, was the only personal war charm obtained. Indeed, the Sauk seem to prefer the large war bundles rather than the small individual charms used by others of the Central tribes, such as the miniature war clubs and lacrosse sticks, etc., which the Menomini and Potawatomi, for example, frequently carry on their persons for protection.

Another object of interest, connected with the use of the sacred bundles that were obtained from the Sauk, is a small reed mat of plain design obtained from an Indian named Fred Grant, another son of the late Mêshê'bêkwa. It was hung up with the sacred bundles of the Wolf gens, and was spread in the host's place in the lodge for him to sit on while the guests feasted at gens ceremonies.

The host sat in the rear of the lodge in the place of honor on this mat, facing the east, with the gens bundles open and spread out before him. Three assistants sat beside him, and neither he nor they took part in the eating of the feast, but sang the sacred songs until he saw the first streaks of dawn in the eastern sky. When this occurred, the host threw back his head and howled like a wolf, after which his followers joined in a chorus of howls.

EXPLANATION OF PLATE II.

TYPICAL SAUK WAR BUNDLES.

Figure 1. Charging bundle of the Wolf gens. Catalog number 30432.
Length 17¾ inches.

Figure 2. Ordinary war bundle, Wolf gens. Catalog number 30406
Length 17 inches.

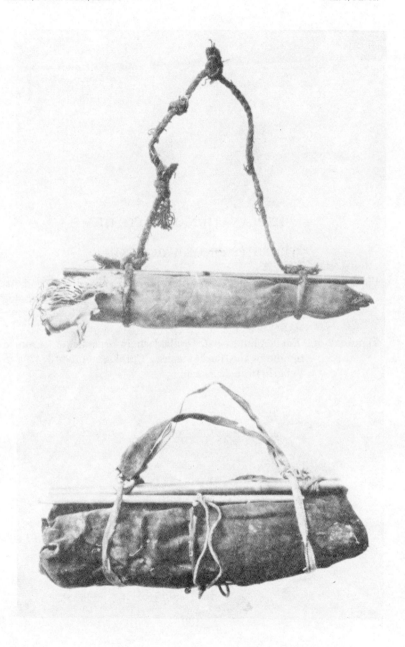

EXPLANATION OF PLATE III.

TROPHIES FROM WAR BUNDLES.

Figure 1.   Quilled war belt with wolf tail and raven feather pendant. From a bundle of the Bear-potato gens. Catalog number 30779a. Length 32 inches.

Figures 2-5.   Eagle plumes with quilled shaft ornaments. From a bundle of the Turkey gens. Catalog number 30436a-d Length 15 inches each.

EXPLANATION OF PLATE IV.

MEDICINE OTTERSKINS FROM A BUNDLE OF THE BEAR-
POTATO GENS.

Figure 1.   Skin of a large otter with wisps of 18 human scalps attached.   Catalog number 30504.   Length 23 inches.

Figure 2.   Skin of a small otter with wisps of 8 human scalps attached.   Catalog number 30505.   Length 16 inches.

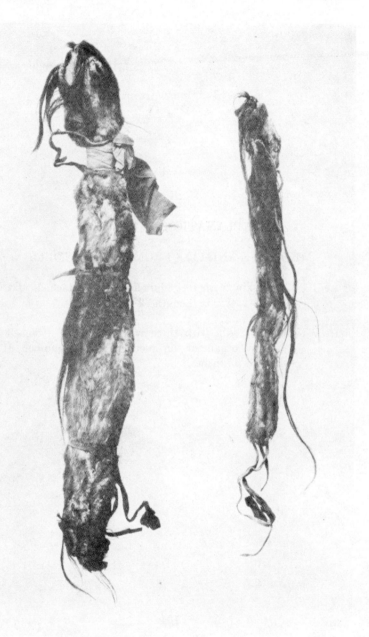

EXPLANATION OF PLATE V.

MEDICINE ANIMALS FROM WAR BUNDLES.

Figure 1. Beaverskin, with forty human scalps attached. Catalog
number 31806. Length 32 inches.

Figure 2. Otter (?) skin with three wisps of scalps attached and
quilled ornament on feet. Catalog number 31796.
Length 33 inches.

EXPLANATION OF PLATE VI.

WAR KILTS FROM BUNDLES.

Figure 1.   Deerskin war kilt from a bundle of the Turkey gens. Catalog number 30459.   Length 22 inches.

Figure 2.   Deerskin war kilt with porcupine quilled ornaments and buffalo tail pendant.   From a bundle of the Turkey gens.   Catalog number 30439.   Length 19 inches.

EXPLANATION OF PLATE VII.

WAR TROPHIES AND AMULETS.

Figure 1.   Headdress of raven skin. Catalog number 31801. Length 12 inches.

Figure 2.   Headdress of hawk skin. Quilled wing strips. Catalog number 31705. Length 23 inches.

Figure 3.   Buffalo horn headdress, imitation wampum headband. From a war bundle of the Wolf gens. Catalog number 31668. Length 22 inches.

Figure 4.   Hawkskin headdress. Quilled wing strips. Catalog number 31720. Length 21½ inches.

Figure 5.   Quilled war kilt. Catalog number 31645. Length as shown, 19 inches.

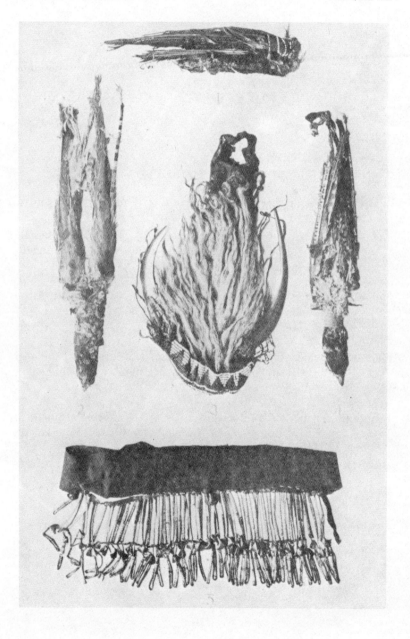

EXPLANATION OF PLATE VIII.

EXCEPTIONAL AMULETS FROM SAUK WAR BUNDLES.

Figure 1.   Quilled buffalo-tail head ornament.   From a war bundle of the Wolf gens.   Catalog number 30407b.   Length 13 inches.

Figure 2.   Quilled buffalo-tail armband.   From a war bundle of the Wolf gens.   Catalog number 30383.   Length 17½ inches.

Figure 3.   Quilled buffalo-tail head ornament.   From a bundle of the Bear-Potato gens.   Catalog number 30780.   Length 9 inches.

Figure 4.   Thong and quill netted garter or belt.   From a bundle of the Turkey gens.   Catalog number 30435.   Length 39 inches.

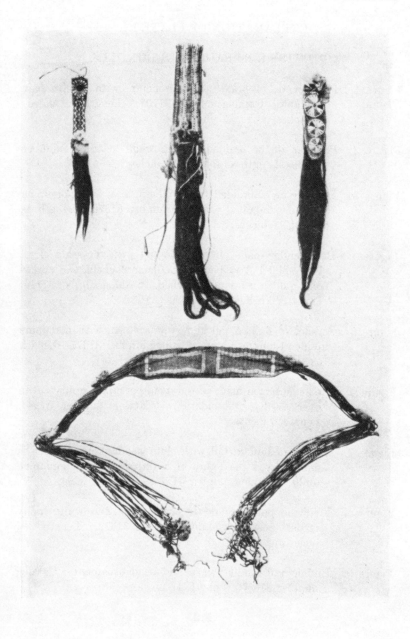

EXPLANATION OF PLATE IX.

OBJECTS FROM SAUK WAR BUNDLES.

Figure 1. Prisoner tie of braided Indian hemp, with human hair pendant. Catalog number 31702. Length, as folded, 20 inches.

Figure 2. Prisoner tie of braided buffalo wool. Catalog number 31800. Length as folded, 16 inches.

Figure 3. Prisoner tie of braided Indian hemp fibre, with porcupine quilled pendants. Catalog number 31670. Length as folded, 16 inches.

Figure 4. Belt amulet made of a buffalo tail with the scalp of an Ivory-billed Woodpecker, medicine packets, and porcupine quilled pendants attached. Catalog number 31714. Length 16 inches.

Figure 5. Amulet of buffalo tail and swan's down, with porcupine quilled thong pendants. Catalog number 31677. Length as shown 14 inches.

Figure 6. Medicine pouch made of red dyed porcupine quills woven over a thong foundation. Catalog number 31684. Length 3 inches.

Figure 7. Amulet of buffalo tail with cloth pendant upon which is embroidered the figure of a thunderbird in porcupine quills. Catalog number 31715. Length 8 inches.

Figure 8. Medicine pouch made of coarse blue and white 'pony trader' beads. Catalog number 31672. Length 2½ inches.

Figure 9. Buffalo tail amulet, yarn and bead ornament. Catalog number 31657. Length 17 inches.

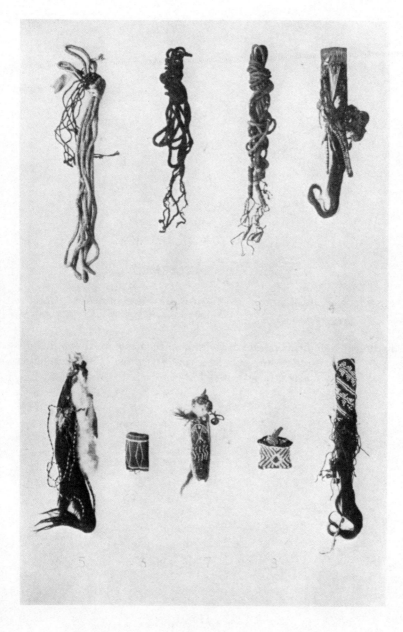

EXPLANATION OF PLATE X.

SAUK WAR CHARMS.

Figure 1.   Warrior's necklace of sweet grass and otter fur.   Catalog
number 30500.   Length 61 inches.

Figure 2.   Medicine packet of the skin of the leg of an albino buffalo.
From a war bundle of the Wolf gens.   Catalog number
3068a.   Length 18½ inches.

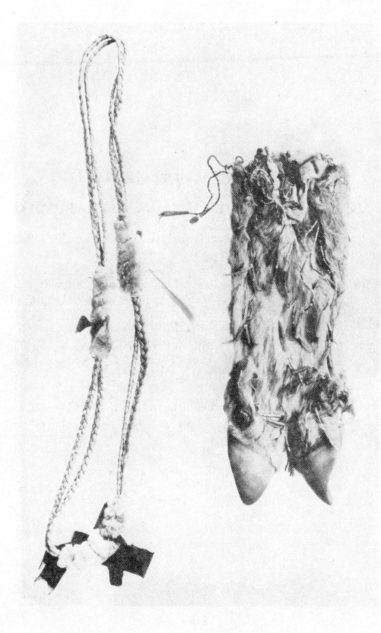

EXPLANATION OF PLATE XI.

PART OF THE CONTENTS OF A KICKAPOO WAR BUNDLE.

Figure 1.   Carved antler medicine spatula.   Catalog number 30833. Length $4\frac{7}{8}$ inches.

Figure 2.   Prisoner tie of Indian hemp, with false embroidery in dyed deer hair.   Catalog number 30836.   Length 25 inches as folded.

Figure 3.   Weasel skin amulet with rattlesnake rattles and a portion of a human scalp attached to the nose.   Catalog number 30838.   Length 15 inches.

Figure 4.   Ordinary form of Indian hemp prisoner tie with porcupine quilled ornaments.   Catalog number 30837.   Length 17 inches, as folded.

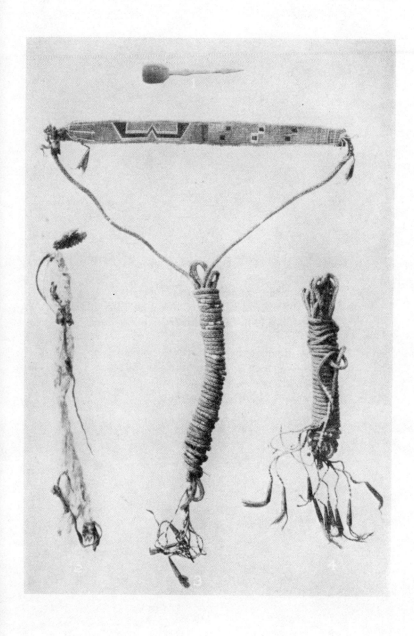

EXPLANATION OF PLATE XII.

ANCIENT STONE-HEADED WAR ARROWS.

Figures 1 and 3. Stone-tipped arrows formerly the property of
Mêshê'bêkwa, a Sauk of the Wolf gens. Catalog numbers 30243a-b. Length $27\frac{7}{8}$ inches.

Figure 2. Stone-tipped arrow formerly the property of a man of the
Wolf gens. Catalog number 30246. Length $30\frac{7}{8}$
inches.

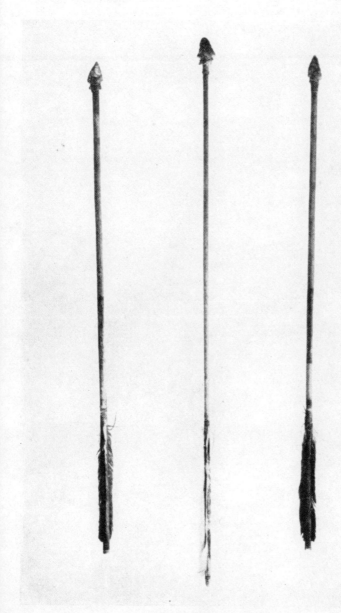

BULLETIN

OF THE

PUBLIC MUSEUM OF THE CITY OF MILWAUKEE

Vol. 5, No. 3, pp. 119–180, Plates 13–26   October 3, 1925

Observations on the Ethnology of the Sauk Indians

Part III, NOTES ON MATERIAL CULTURE

By

Alanson Skinner

Observations on the Ethnology of the Sauk Indians
Part III, Notes on Material Culture

CONTENTS

ILLUSTRATIONS

Plates

INTRODUCTION

Generally speaking, the material culture of the Sauk was closely similar to that of the other Central tribes, that is the Fox, Kickapoo, Potawatomi, Menomini, and Winnebago, finding its closest relationship with that of the Fox. In fact, Sauk and Fox material cultures seem to be nearly identical in many details. Resembling the Sauk also in this respect were the tribes of the Miami-Peoria-Illinois group. The Southern Siouans, the Ioway and Oto, Osage, and even the Caddoan Pawnee, wore articles actually obtained from the Sauk or made in imitation of them by their own less skillful hands.

It is certain that at the time of the first arrival of white explorers, when the Sauk were still situated close to the Great Lakes, they shared the maritime culture of the Ojibway and Menomini, and were great users of birchbark. With their withdrawal westward across the Mississippi they came more and more under prairie Indian influence. The horse fell into their possession, for Peter Pond says in his journal that[1]: "Sometimes they Go Near St. Fee in New Mexico and Bring with them Spanish Horseis. I have seen meney of them." With the horse they took over a number of features of horse culture that are not found among all the Central tribes; for example, the use of the elkhorn-handled quirt. It is quite probable that the Winnebago and Menomini may have received the horse and such features of cavalry culture as they possess through the Sauk.

It was the original intention of the writer of these notes to amplify them by further research in the field, and by a visit to the closely related Meskwaki or Fox. Since circumstances have prevented this it has been decided to publish them as they are, with the hope that they will supercede, in a slight degree, the general lack of printed data on the Sauk. The articles that are here figured are those in the possession of the Public Museum of the City of Milwaukee, collected in Oklahoma and Kansas by the writer in 1922 and 1923. Other Sauk material, gathered by Mr. M. R. Harrington, is in the Museum of the American Indian, Heye Foundation, at New York. Meskwaki collections are to be found in the Field Museum at Chicago, and the American Museum of Natural History at New York, and especially, in the private collection of Mr. Milford G. Chandler of Chicago. All of these collections will well repay further study.

---

[1]Pond, Peter, Journal, 1740-75. Wisconsin Hist. Coll., Vol. XVIII, p. 335, Madison, 1908.

LODGE TYPES

For summer use the Sauk made large square houses of elm bark with ridged roofs. Those observed by the writer were of unusual size, hence considerably larger than those of the Menomini, often measuring forty to fifty feet in length and thirty to thirty-five feet in breadth. Although it is now difficult for the Oklahoma Sauk to obtain bark, some of these houses are still to be seen (plate XIII, fig. 1), usually closely adjacent to their comfortable modern frame buildings. Other houses of exactly similar type are now built of planks and sometimes even these have a bark roof. They are used as places of residence by the older and more conservative people, as ceremonial meeting places, as storage rooms for sacred bundles, and the like.

About a yard above the floor, on each side, a broad platform extends the full length of the lodge. It is spread with reed mats, and is used both for storage of household utensils and as sleeping and sitting quarters. The rafters are cluttered with mats of cattail flags used to cover the winter lodge and other utensils. In the northwest end (in some cases at least) hang the sacred bundles. The relatively narrow passageway can be used for a fire in bad weather, but most of the cooking is done out of doors, if necessary, under a bough arbor.

These large square houses are called *anagawikan* (*-wikanan*). Formerly several related families lived in each. Certainly, as observed above, they are unusually large buildings for the Central tribes, and suggest the possibility of Iroquois influence, although such sizable residences were occasionally used by the Central Algonkians. In this connection it must not be forgotten that an entire village of Meskwaki (Fox) was once moved bodily to central New York by the Seneca Iroquois, and, while many were absorbed by that tribe, others returned to Wisconsin after a period of years and may well have carried Iroquoian ideas back to their old homes.

For winter use, the Sauk preferred the usual Algonkian round wigwam made of cattail flag mats, and called by them *pûkwe'gan*, (plate XIII, fig. 2). Small houses of this type, for the seclusion of women during their periods, may be seen today adjoining the residence of many families, even some not otherwise conservative. In late May, 1922, several dome-shaped lodges were in use near Cushing, Oklahoma, although most families had abandoned them for the summer and moved into the square wigwams.

All lodges should be set up with the door to the east, the square lodges, having a rear door facing the west. In Sauk the door is called *skua'täm*, the fireplace *awasiu pota'wan* or "warming place."

Each of the four corner posts of a square lodge has its name as follows: the east post is called *wätcimo'kahak* "where daylight appears;" the west post *wätcipûgê'shimuk*, "where the sun goes down;" the north post is entitled *wajina'kwäk*, or "noon;" and the south post *wäjigäsiû'k*. The scaffolds are called *ota'sanûn*.

Winter villages were situated in the sheltered bends of streams, where the people remained until about the middle of April, when they went to their summer farms.

There is inferential evidence that, even in early days, the bark houses of the Sauk were of unusual size for members of the Central tribes. Jonathan Carver, writing of his travels in 1766[2], says: "On the 8th of October we got our canoes into the Wisconsin River, which at this place is more than a hundred yards wide; and the next day arrived at the Great Town of the Saukies. This is the largest and best built Indian town I ever saw. It contains about ninety houses, each large enough for several families. These are built of hewn plank, neatly joined, and covered with bark so compactly as to keep out the most penetrating rains. Before the doors are placed comfortable sheds, in which the inhabitants sit, when the weather will permit, and smoke their pipes. The streets are regular and spacious; so that it appears more like a civilized town, than the abode of savages."

As Carver had recently visited the towns of the Winnebago and Menomini, and was quite familiar with Indian lodges in general, it is evident that his account that the village was large and well built and the houses big enough to shelter several families was not the haphazard remark of an unseasoned observer. His statement that the houses were of hewn plank covered with bark is, however, unquestionably a slip of the tongue or a poor observation, probably the former. The houses were without doubt merely built of bark slabs as is, and was, the universal custom in the Woodlands. The Sauk still use sheds or arbors like those mentioned by Carver, attached, or adjacent to, their Oklahoma residences.

On the other hand, Peter Pond[3], in his journal, written a few years subsequent to Carver's visit, remarks on the use of planks, though he possibly refers to square beams, judging by the context, and also testifies to the extraordinary size of the Sauk houses at this same

[2]Carver, Jonathan, "Three Years Travels Through the Interior Parts of North America, etc.," Philadelphia, 1796, p. 29.
[3]Pond, Peter, Ibid: p. 335.

village. He says: "Thare Villeag is Bilt Cheafely with Plank thay Hugh Out of Wood—that is ye upright—the top is Larch (arched) Over with Strong Sapplins Sufficient to Support the Roof and Covered with Barks which Makes them a tile roof. Sum of thare Huts are Sixtey feet long and Contanes Several fammalayes. Thay Rase a Platfoarm on Each Side of thare Huts About two feet high and about five feet Broad on which they Seat & Sleap. Thay have no flores But Bild Thar fire on the Ground in the Midel of the Hut and have a Hole threw the Ruf for the Smoke to Pas."

There is a possibility that the Sauk of this period may have been able to obtain planks from the white traders, but this seems very doubtful. At the present time many of the Oklahoma Sauk substitute planks for the bark covering of their lodges, otherwise built in the old fashion.

It seems more probable that Carver had reference to axe-squared upright posts or beams, used in house construction, which he, through a slip of the pen, or, perhaps, due to a change in usage of the term, called planks, and Pond, who remarks several times on his familiarity with Carver's journal, fell into the same terminology through his recollection of Carver's description.

Painted tipis made of buffalo hide were constructed for winter use, after the Sauk moved into the prairie country. Details concerning their structure were not obtainable, as they have long been out of use.

COSTUMES

MEN'S GARMENTS

In former years the dress of the men of the Sauk tribe was the most gorgeous of all the Central Algonkians, yet it conformed to the general ancient patterns widely spread among the forest Indians.

Men formerly wore, as they do still on rare occasions, fillets or head bands made of the fur of wildcats, bears, squirrels, or, for ceremonies and especially dressy functions, otter. Those of bear fur were made of the skin of the animal's neck, where the hair grows most luxuriantly. When otter was used, sometimes the entire skin was taken and folded over to make a head band. Again, a simple strip of the fur was used, ornamented along the upper edge with scarlet cloth or a strip of beadwork, and with beaded medallions at intervals. An especially elaborate variety (plate XIV, fig. 1), added to these features the entire skin of a second otter with the legs trimmed off. This was folded over to make it narrower and attached to the rear as a pendant or trailer. This like the head bands was also adorned with bead medallions and a longitudinal band of silk applique or beadwork, attached where the two sides of the folded skin came together.

Two old otter fur headdresses were collected in war bundles of the Turkey Gens. In these the skin is apparently cut narrower and sewed together at intervals with buckskin thongs, and tiny leather bags bound to it hold war medicines. These are ornamented with scarlet down and metallic jinglers.

Headdresses were made of hawkskin with short otter fur streamers and owl and hawkskins were also split and worn with the bird's head over the forehead. Several different types of buffalo headdresses were known. One which was collected is a mere strip of fur taken from the head of a buffalo calf, retaining the nubby spike horns, one of which is painted with red ochre, the other being left in its natural black. This headdress was evidently bound transversely across the head, and tied on under the chin so that the horns stood upright on the wearer's head. It was taken from a war bundle of the Wolf Gens. A more elaborate form consists of two split buffalo horns attached to a fabric (red flannel) headcovering, fringed in the rear. Across the forehead passes a broad band decorated with coarse porcupine quillwork. There is also a fringe of deer's hair dyed scarlet. This headdress was in a bundle of the Deer Gens, and has been damaged by fire, so was probably saved from the Sauk village in Oklahoma when burned some years ago by Government orders because of infection from a smallpox epidemic.

Buffalo headdresses of a still more elaborate character are said to be used in the performance of the buffalo dance, but none were seen.

Besides these fur fillets, the dyed deer's hair, turkey or porcupine bristle roach was also highly prized. It was skillfully woven by hand of one or more of the materials named, with usually an outer fringe of natural black hair and was kept carefully rolled upon a stick till wanted. Such roaches are now so highly valued owing to the amounts which the neighboring Osage are willing to pay for them, that, while a few were seen, none could be obtained from the Sauk. However, a specimen from the Fox of Tama, Iowa, exactly similar to the Sauk type, is shown in plate XVI, fig. 7. The roach is attached to the head by passing the scalp lock through a small aperture left in the broad or upper end of the roach for that purpose, and running a small wooden peg through the narrow braid. These roaches were noted among tribes as far east as the Atlantic coast by many of the early writers.

They are kept open by a spreader carved of elk antler, plate XVI, fig. 7, which is often elaborately ornamented with carved designs. To the smaller end of the spreader is attached a bone tube, at the base of which is a spike upon which is impaled an eagle plume, which revolves upon its pivot in the breeze. The plume itself often bears a beautiful shaft ornament, plate XVI, figs. 6 and 8, which is made of carefully wound porcupine quills, or, as in later examples, horse hair. War plumes were sometimes dyed scarlet, and to the tips of the eagle feathers tufts of scarlet colored down, bits of white ermine fur and rattlesnake rattles were often attached. A deerskin cap covered with split hawk, owl and eagle feathers was obtained at Nemaha, Kansas.

Sometimes the warriors wore no headdress other than their own carefully roached hair, the head being shorn except for a ridge that passed from forehead to nape, with the narrow braid of the scalp lock cultivated at the crown. Often again a man added the deer hair roach to his own bristling locks, and even then sometimes wore a fillet of fur. His social and military standing were evident in the number of his eagle plumes, each proclaiming a coup or blow struck against the enemy.

Facial and body painting was frequent, the commonest sort being the white or black pigment denoting the moiety, Oskû'sh or Kî'shko, of the wearer. This has been largely discarded in recent years.

The ears were pierced for pendants of wampum or metallic earbobs, and necklaces of wampum were employed. Other necklaces were made of cylindrical bone or shell beads, tapering towards the ends (commonly called "wampum pipes," "hair pipes" and, by archeologists, for they are found on historic sites in the east, "baldric beads"). These were strung in two transverse parallel rows, hanging down on the breast, or strung end for end in more usual necklace form. As these beads seem to be wholly of white origin, and were obtained by the Indians from the traders, no further notice need be given them. Necklaces or bands woven of yarn and beads to which medicines in small leather bags are attached are found in many war bundles.

Wolf skins were slit so that they could be put over the head, with the head of the wolf hanging over the breast and the tail pendant down the back. They were especially worn by warriors of the Wolf Gens.

Collars of scarlet colored deer hair, made somewhat like the roaches but thinner, were also used.

The favorite necklace of the Sauk, however, is that made of the long yellow striped claws of the grizzly bear and otter fur. These are of two varieties, the commoner of which is composed of claws strung through perforations near the base on a foundation of cloth or skin which is closely wrapped with otter fur cut in strips. Each claw has a second perforation midway to the point, by which it is strung again, and they are held separate at this point by means of large globular glass beads, often of blue color. A pendant composed of the entire skin of an otter hangs down the back, and this is adorned, as is often the rest of the necklace, with beaded medallions attached at intervals. The other type has a similar appearance to the first, except that the otterskin between the claws, instead of being wrapped spirally about the foundation, is folded over it lengthwise and sewed together beneath. An example of this type, from the Fox of Tama, Iowa, is shown in plate XIV, fig. 3. Twenty to forty claws are needed to make such a necklace.

These grizzly bear claw necklaces are now not only very rare, but exceedingly prized by the Sauk, who can scarcely be induced to part with one. In fact, none was found by the writer in Oklahoma in 1922, although undoubtedly some existed. In recent years the Osage have bought them at enormous prices, and they are greatly desired by all the neighboring tribes, such as the Pawnee, Ioway, Oto, and Ponca. In former times, they were not only regarded as beautiful ornaments, but were prized because of the difficulty of obtaining the claws, even when grizzly bears were abundant. An old Sauk once told the writer that they had but two ways of obtaining the coveted talons. The first, and most obvious way, was to journey to the parts of the plains where grizzlies were then abundant, daring hostile tribes and risking their lives in slaying the formidable animals. The other was to venture into the country of the Santee Dakota and there find and kill a Dakota warrior who had a necklace of the plain strung claws, an exploit no less dangerous than the former. A grizzly bear claw necklace, therefore, silently proclaimed to all who saw it that its wearer was a man and a warrior of distinction.

Similar necklaces are reported to have been worn by the Menomini in ancient times as the especial insignia of the braves and, indeed, the writer has collected among this people a few individual claws showing the double perforation characteristic of this type of necklace. The Menomini personal name Oskû'sh, which means literally, "A claw," is often translated as meaning "Brave." It seems probable therefore, that the wearers of these necklaces were popularly called "Claws," just as the dome-shaped mat wigwams of the tribe were often called simply "mats." Something of the same significance seems to attach itself to the Sauk tribal moiety called likewise "Oskû'sh," who were not supposed to falter or turn back in any undertaking, especially in war. Bear claw necklaces of this type have been noted among the Fox, Menomini, Ioway, Oto, Osage, Pawnee, and Arikara.

Little is known or remembered about native-made shirts. Old people say that perhaps these were not worn in the earliest times, a buffalo robe, or the skin of a bear, wolf, or wildcat being thrown over the shoulder on the windward side, as among the Algonkians of the Atlantic Coast. For ceremonial purposes, even up to recent years, the warriors of the Sauk often went naked to the waist, the grizzly claw necklace being regarded as sufficient dress. In the years subsequent to the removal of the tribe across the Mississippi deerskin shirts, made in imitation of those of the Plains tribes, were sometimes used.

Breech cloths are now made of broadcloth, strips about four feet long and from a foot to eighteen inches wide being passed between the legs and allowed to fall over the belt in front and rear. The outer sides of these flaps are embroidered with conventional floral or scroll figures, as is shown in plate XVI, fig. 11. This type was formerly made of tanned deerskin embroidered with the dyed quills of the porcupine. The Sauk ridicule their Mêskwaki' relatives because they declare that the latter wear only an apron flap in front and expose the bare buttocks behind. Nevertheless in two of the war bundles of the Turkey Gens collected by the writer in Oklahoma, aprons of exactly this type occur. These are shown in plate VI, figs. 1 and 2, in this volume, Part II, and are ancient pieces ornamented with porcupine quill work in simple bars and crosses of yellow, black and red. One has an elaborate buffalo tail pendant in front and both are fringed and have metallic jinglers made from bits of old trade brass and copper kettles. In cold weather the old time Sauk men wore breech cloths of the tanned skins of the raccoon. They relate that when they dwelt in their old homes in Wisconsin, where it is much colder than in Oklahoma or Kansas, they were obliged to turn the fur side in in winter to keep their testicles from freezing. The same statement was made to the writer by Eastern Cree residing on Hudson Bay who use loin cloths woven of twisted strips of rabbit fur for the same purpose.

An example of the hip length leggings of the general Woodland style still worn by the men, is shown in plate XV, fig. 2. Another type, now obsolete, was made like the leg of a modern white-man's drawers, but skin tight and with flaps expanding at the base to cover the foot. This sort was fringeless. Another type had a narrow beaded or quilled strip along the seam, which was worn in front, and a short pendant flap above or at the knee, which was ornamented. This type was frequently fringed with locks taken from the scalps of enemies. Similar leggings were once in vogue among the Fox, Kickapoo, and Winnebago.

Garters were woven of yarn, yarn and beads, or beads alone, and were worn outside the leggings below the knees. Some of these are shown in plate XVI, figs. 10 and 12. Another type, found also among the Ioway, was of otter fur with a square beaded medallion pendant at one end, and a longer one, the shape of the otter's tail at the other. A pair of these was found by the writer in Oklahoma and is illustrated in plate XV, fig. 3.

Beaded belts were also made (plate XV, fig. 1), and were worn around the waist or over the shoulders, as were the beaded shoulder pouches or bandoliers, shown in plate XVII, fig. 2. Yarn sashes of several weaves were worn as turbans around the head, or as shoulder or waist belts (plate XVII, figs. 1 and 3).

Moccasins had soft soles of one piece with the uppers, as is customary everywhere in the Woodlands. They were made with a seam running over the instep backward from the toe, and with huge ankle flaps that were decorated heavily with quill or beadwork. Plate XVI, figs. 1, 2, 3, 4, 5, and 9, show examples of Sauk moccasins, and it will be noted that the decorations on the flaps are not bilaterally symmetrical. That is, each flap of the same moccasin has a different design, but the designs are duplicated on the corresponding part of the other moccasin of the pair. The designs nowadays run to small geometric figures, preferably diamonds or triangles, but formerly floral scrolls prevailed on one of the flaps of each shoe. This custom is found elsewhere only among the Fox and Kickapoo.

GLOSSARY OF NATIVE TERMS

Fur fillet	*pêshi'magwe*
Otter fur fillet	*pêmitênikûn*
Otter fur fillet with trailer	*kätotäwo'ia*
Deer hair roach	*wawiᵡäpê'nwan*

Wampum	*pi'ismikuk*
Bone or wampum pipe beads	*shoska'gûnwûk*
Deerskin shirt	*asái pisäka*
Deerskin leggings	*matäte'han*
Leggings with hanging flap	*anêshátähan*
Breech cloth	*näpane'a'sian*
Wolf skin shoulder throw	*nipigo'skahut*
Belt	*kêtcip^w*
Garters	*nägakiga'pihûk*

WOMEN'S GARMENTS

It is said that in ancient times the Sauk women wore two piece dresses, in winter the waist being made of raccoon skin and sleeveless, but in summer of thin tanned deerskin. Bearskin robes served as blankets and skirts. The summer skirt was made of thin dressed fawnskin, and, while some are said to have been beautified with painted designs like those on the leathern trunks, others were ornamented along the front and bottom borders with bands of porcupine quill embroidery, or even strips of woven quill work.

Although the deerskin shirt or waist was sometimes worn by the women in summer, in hot weather, at least, they often went naked above the waist except for a necklace plaited of inner basswood bark, and painted red, so worn as to cover the breasts. In ancient times their headdress was merely plaited leathern thongs.

Marrow from the shin bone of the deer was used for hair oil. The bones were broken open and heated until the marrow melted and ran. Skunk oil was also used on the head to expel lice.

In more recent times, that is, since the coming of the whites into their country, materials of white-man's manufacture have taken the place of most of the old stuffs used by the women of the Central tribes for their dress. The garments of the women of the Sauk were extremely similar in appearance to those of the Fox, Menomini, Miami, Winnebago, Ioway, Oto, Osage, Ponca, Omaha, Santee Sioux, Wyandot and several other tribes. The waist was of calico and was usually ornamented with brooches of silver or flash metal. The skirt was made of a square piece of broadcloth of black, blue, or scarlet, ornamented along the bottom and side borders with silk ribbon applique, and wrapped around the waist, where it was held in place by means of a belt, but was allowed to remain open in front or at one side (plate XVIII, figs. 1 and 3). The leggings were of the same material handsomely beaded (plate XVIII, figs. 2 and 4) and of knee length, being held below the knee by a plain string garter. The moccasins were like those of the men, except for size, but were, perhaps, less boldly ornamented. Necklaces of strung beads and silver or flash metal earbobs were commonly worn. The hair was braided in a single plait and folded back, being then wrapped in an oblong cloth wrapper, the ends of which bore rectangular beaded ornaments. From the center depended a long streamer of beautiful beadwork, often woven on the bias. In plate XIX, figs. 1-8, may be seen typical examples of these hair ornaments.

GLOSSARY OF NATIVE TERMS

Woman's raccoonskin waist	ä'sipunê pi'säka
Deerskin skirt	asaiêko'tä
Broadcloth skirt	mûnito'waigan
Deerskin moccasins	asa'i makä'sinûn
Hair dress (cloth part)	aˣpaˣho'n
Hair dress (bead trailers)	nishägipû'nwan

HOUSEHOLD UTENSILS

In ancient times, and even down to the present, the mortar and pestle for pounding corn were indispensible parts of the equipment of every primitive family. The usual Central Algonkian style of mortar is constructed from the horizontal short section of a log, hollowed by fire, and with two lugs or handles, one at each end. It is probable that the Sauk formerly used this type, instead of the vertical form employed in the East and Southeast. However, the variety in vogue today is the vertical sort, with a pestle having a heavy and considerably enlarged upper end (plate XXII, figs. 1 and 3). The Central Algonkian pestle is usually rather light, short, and double-ended, giving it a modified "dumb-bell" style. The type of both the mortar and pestle, now used by the Sauk, is decidedly southeastern, resembling those in use among the Muskhogean peoples, and doubtless was derived from the neighboring Creek and Yuchi of Oklahoma.

Formerly buffalo rawhide trunks, like those still used by the Meskwaki, were commonly found among the Sauk. An exhaustive search revealed only one among the Oklahoma contingent in 1922 and

1923. It is shown in plate XXII, fig. 4. In spite of the declaration of the old Sauk at Cushing that these trunks were made for them by the Ioway and Osage, the method of shaping them by clever folding, and the painted designs are utterly different from those used by the southern Siouans, and similar, if not identical with the methods of the Meskwaki, Kickapoo and other Central Algonkians. A buffalo hide trunk is called *nano'swa muski'mutä.*

Wooden bowls and spoons (plate XXII, fig. 2, and plate XXIII, figs. 1-12) are still commonly used, although more often for ceremonial than ordinary occasions. Although sometimes well made and bearing handles with human effigies upon them, the bowls and ladles or spoons of the Sauk are not as a rule as skillfully fashioned as those of the average Central Algonkian tribe.

Mats made of reeds were and still are used as floor and bench coverings in Sauk wigwams. Plate XXIV, fig. 2, shows a typical example, while plate XXIV, fig. 1, reproduces a photograph of a Meskwaki effigy mat, a close inspection of which will bring to light the conventionalized figures of four underworld panthers.

INDUSTRIES

TANNING

A deerhide is first soaked in water two or three days. Then it is thrown over the upper end of a split log driven obliquely into the ground, which comes about waist high and is carefully smoothed over the rounded portion. The hair is then removed by scraping with a drawshave-like implement or beaming tool called *plê'shkwäkikunau.* A wooden handle with a horizontal metal blade is now used. The skin is then turned inside out by reversing it, and the adhering flesh is taken off in the same manner.

Next the hide is soaked in warm water mixed with deer's brains— the brains having previously been boiled in the water—where it is allowed to stand all night. In the morning the skin is taken out of the brain water and wrung out by twisting it around a post or sapling by means of a wooden spatula used as a tourniquet or lever. It is then stretched on a rectangular form, called *mänê'sêtcikun,* by means of cords or thongs passed through holes at intervals along the borders. These cords are termed *pish'akûnûn.* While on the stretching frame, it is rubbed all day with the blade of the wooden spatula.

Next day the edges are trimmed, and it is folded over to make a bag which is sewed up along the side where the edges come together. In this condition it is held with the opening down over a shallow hole in which a smoky fire made of sumach or cottonwood is built, the upper end being fastened in the elevated crotch of a split stick driven obliquely in the ground, and the border of the mouth of the bag pegged down. In one or two hours the smoke has saturated the skin and it is done and ready for use in garments, and so forth. Very little of this work is now done by the Sauk, who rely almost wholly upon the Kickapoo for their supply of tanned deerskin; the Mexican band of Kickapoo being able to obtain deer in their place of voluntary exile.

WOODWORKING

The Sauk say that their ancient grooved stone axes were very dull, and made the work of cutting down trees laborious. They were forced to hack continuously at the same place, and it took a whole day to sever a knot suitable for making a bowl.

Fire was the active agent, which they say they employed in work of this sort. The trees were felled by first burning, then hacking out the charcoal, then applying fire again. When at length the tree was down, it was cut in sections suitable for making canoes or mortars by similar means.

When a section was intended for a canoe, the next step was to level off the bark on the upper surface as much as possible with the stone axe. Then hot coals were laid along its length, and when these had died out, the charred wood was scraped away with a mussel shell, the process being continued *ad infinitum* until the log was hollowed. It was also shaped in the same way.

For firewood, bark and such dry limbs as could be battered off were used. The old Sauk maintain that sometimes a broken stone having a sharp fracture was far more efficacious for wood working than one of their carefully made grooved axes.

NATIVE DYES

Yellow: Obtained by boiling articles to be colored, such as reeds, with the roots of the sour dock (*Rhumex acetosella*).

Black and dark blue: Obtained in the same manner from black walnut bark (*Juglans nigra*).

Red: Likewise obtained from the blood-root (*Sanguenaria canadensis*).

Green: This color is said to have been obtained from the whites, and not to have been an aboriginal dye. The same is true of most shades of blue.

In digging all roots for dyes or medicines, the Sauk placed tobacco in the hole whence the root was taken, with thanks to our earth mother whose hairs they are.

VEGETABLE FIBRES USED IN BAG MAKING

The Sauk were familiar with the following fibres from which they made twine for bags, etc.

Nettle called *a'sa*^{x}*piäk*

Basswood inner bark, called *wikopinu*

Cedar inner bark, called *mêskwa'*^{wa}

In plate XXI, are shown a number of typical Sauk woven yarn and vegetable fibre bags of characteristic designs. The two broad faces almost invariably bear entirely different designs.

TRANSPORTATION

CANOES, SNOWSHOES, PACKSTRAPS

Canoes were made generally of trees felled with fire and stone axes, shaped and hollowed by burning and scraping with mussel shells as described in an earlier section. Boats were also made of hickory and yellow elm bark sewed with basswood. The seams were caulked with shredded slippery elm bark fibre and pitch. If the Sauk ever had birch bark canoes, these have been completely forgotten. Doubtless none have been seen among them since they were expelled from the Green Bay, Wisconsin, region by the Menomini. Elm bark canoes were called *wikopimish*.

Round "bull-boats" of buffalo hide stretched over a bowl-shaped wooden framework, were made in later times for crossing prairie rivers. Someone swam ahead and pulled the boat by a thong held between the teeth.

The Sauk elders have only the vaguest memories of snowshoes. These, too, have become obsolete since their migration from their northern homes.

Packstraps of leather, for carrying burdens on the back, the strap passing over the forehead, are still sometimes used, especially by old women gathering wood.

Cradle boards of the general Central Algonkian type, with movable foot boards, were used to carry children. They were made from the wood of living trees, just as are the falsefaces of the Iroquois. The idea seems to be that of a sympathetic connection between the life of the tree and that of the child. Cradle boards made of cut or seasoned wood, or of white-man's boards, are deemed unlucky.

VEGETAL FOODS

GARDEN PRODUCTS

Pumpkins (wa'pîkonun) are eaten when cut in chunks and boiled. They are also cut in circular slices and the slices braided, dried and suspended over poles for storage. Dried pumpkins are called *wápihon.*

Maize. Sweet corn, *wisko'pimînûk,* is eaten green after boiling or roasting in the embers. It is also prepared by parboiling, drying over night and scraping from the cob with a mussel shell, the left valve of the animal being most convenient for the use of the ordinary right-handed person. It is then dried on mats spread in the hot sun on the ground. Two days exposure are enough to cure it for winter use. In this condition it is called *pagaswahuk* and is ready to grind with mortar and pestle (*pota'hagûn* and *pota'hagûn hûskwan*) to make corn meal.

When ground, the meal is (or rather was formerly, as sifting baskets are said to exist no longer) sifted with a native-made basket. The coarser part which was retained by the mesh, was used for corn soup, the finer meal was made into dumplings which were boiled in the soup. Hominy is called *tû'kwahan.*

Green corn, while still somewhat milky, is scraped free from the cob with a deer's jaw. A little flour and sugar with an abundance of grease is then added, and it is patted into cakes to be baked in the ashes. These are called *papû'kêna^x.*

Sometimes the scraped green corn, as above described, is mixed with beans, made into loaves, wrapped and tied with cornhusks. The loaves are then dropped into a kettle and boiled for two hours, kept over night to cool, and eaten thereafter. This is regarded as an especially palatable dish, and is called *wiwa'pisut papû'kêna^x* or "Wrapped up bread."

"Lye Hominy," (*panûki'hûk*) is made of shelled corn boiled with "one-half a kettle full" of wood ashes, until the hulls begin to slip.

The corn was then placed in coarse sacks of nettle fibre of open twined weave, which are now said to be obsolete, until freed of lye, when it was ready for eating. Owing to the lack of hulling sacks, lye hominy is seldom made now, as burnt fingers too frequently result.

Raw lye hominy is regarded as a specific against worms in children, and as a general health food. It is more usual, however, to cook it with marrow bones, which greatly add to its palatability.

Parched corn (*kaka'wäsuhûk*) is pounded into meal, and as among many other Indian tribes, it is used as a refreshing stimulent on journeys. About a quart of the sifted meal is carried in a deerskin bag by hunters and warriors, and a few spoonsful or mouthsful taken in water, constitutes enough for a meal. The coarser meal is more used for home eating.

Pop corn, called *papagesuhuk*, is known to, and used by, the Sauk.

Beans. There are five or six varieties of beans recognized by the tribe, and the generic term for this vegetable is *mûskojîs*.

Wild Potatoes. The tuber (*Apios tuberosa*) called "Indian potato" or, in Sauk, *manotäo p'äniäk*, is much used, and one gens is named for the plant which is also called *muko-päniäk* or "bean-potato."

Dried Yellow Water Lily Root, wakepîn or *yakepîn*, is abundantly utilized as food, when boiled.

It goes without saying that all varieties of berries, both fresh, and dried when out of season, are eaten by the Sauk. Naturally under modern conditions the scope of their vegetable diet has been greatly widened. Nuts of all available species are also relished.

SUGAR MAKING

Although it has not been possible for the Sauk to make maple sugar for many years because of their removal from the region where maple trees abounded, some details of the manufacture of the sweet are still remembered. In the late winter or very early spring the Bear gens held a special feast, during which prayers were offered to the Great Spirit for permission to tap the maple trees, four days later. During the intervening time the men busied themselves in making sap spouts of box elder wood, or slippery elm bark, and elm bark receptacles to catch the sap. When all was in readiness the sap was collected and boiled all night. Finally it was all poured into one large receptacle and about one fourth of a pound of beef tallow was added. It was boiled until it reached a stage where it popped when it bubbled. Then some was placed in a knot bowl and stirred with a heavy wooden ladle until it was crystallized. No one was so much as allowed to taste the sugar before all were ready.

When the entire batch of sugar was prepared, a dog feast and thanksgiving ceremony were held before any one partook of the sugar. At length, all being in readiness, eight people were invited to eat out of one large bowl in which a quart of the sugar was placed. This they had to finish without attempting to drink any water. After this all might eat all they desired. Probably this was a form of the usual eating contest between four selected members of each moiety.

Sugar cakes made in moulds as well as powdered sugar were prepared.

Sugar cakes	*Mäsiwä'ahûn*
Maple sugar (Real sugar)	*Pakisi'sêbák*[w]
Maple tree	*Shishikimä'hishá*
Sugar bush	*Sisibákukadjîk*
Elm bark sap receptacle	*Anep onagan*

WILD RICE GATHERING

The Sauk have been so long absent from the wild rice country that they only vaguely remember that it was harvested in canoes with two sticks held in the hands. They have completely forgotten the shelling and winnowing processes. They call wild rice *mûno'min*, and the Menomini Indians they term *Mûnominewê'kajîk*, or "Wild-rice-gatherers," a variant of the Menomini tribal name for themselves.

The Sauk have long been noted as agriculturists. Pond remarks[4] about 1765: "The Women Rase Grate Crops of Corn, Been, Punkens, Potatoes, Millans, and artikels—"

TOBACCO CULTURE

The Sauk throw tobacco seeds on the ground somewhere near the house. They also set on fire a brush pile in the woods, to which they return a few days later and walk over the resultant pile of wood ashes in their bare feet to see if they are cold. If this is the case, they sprinkle the seed on the ashes and let it grow. This is done in May, the tobacco is gathered for use in July and August, some being left for seed.

Native Tobacco is very highly prized for all ceremonial purposes, being much more valuable to the Sauk than "store tobacco."

Both pipes (plate XX, fig. 5) and tobacco pouches (plate XX,

[4]Pond, Peter, Ibid, p. 335.

fig. 2) are now rarely seen among the Sauk. The tobacco pouch figured here is of typical tribal style, and is much more elongated and capacious than those used by the Menomini, Forest Potawatomi, and their other neighbors. In size and shape but not in ornamentation it resembles somewhat more closely the pouches of the various Plains tribes. Native tobacco is called both *anenotawi* and *anenotaowa sama*.

HUNTING AND FISHING

BUFFALO HUNTING

The Sauk in earlier days ventured quite far out on the prairies in pursuit of the buffalo, and their removal from their homes in Wisconsin and Illinois to west of the Mississippi gave an added stimulus to this quest.

In the month of June when the corn and beans had a good start, the whole tribe, with the exception of the old people who remained to watch the crops, went out on the buffalo hunt. When they approached the vicinity in which they expected to find the herds, the leader would attempt to have a prophetic dream which he would report to his head men, who called in the scouts and gave them instructions to kill a few buffalo near at hand so that all the people might have a mouthful. Then the scouts were each given a little tobacco and dismissed.

When the scouts returned successful, "with meat shot with arrows," as the saying is, the leader sang as he saw them approaching with the meat. Next day the camp was moved to within two miles of the main herd.

When on the hunt, the chiefs and the *nänawi'ˣtuwûk*[5] or braves (the latter acted as hunt and camp police) held the people together on the march to prevent straggling, and fixed the location of the camp, (see Marston). The lodges were not pitched in a circle but in a row or straight line. When a herd was located, the warrior-police held the hunters in check until the herd had been circled and all were up wind from the buffalo. The Sauk men were then placed in line ten feet apart. When all was in readiness the signal was given and the charge made on an even basis. An old man was appointed to watch and see that no one beat the starting signal. If any one did, that man was severely beaten by the police after the day's hunt was over.

---

[5]Note the occurrence of this term which is regularly found in Menomini. The usual Sauk term for braves or police is *watâ'säo* which occurs as a personal name in Menomini.

Urging their horses alongside of the fleeing bison, the hunters would rap on their bowstrings with their arrows and cause the herd to scatter so all would have a better chance. They endeavored to drive their arrows through the buffalo's kidneys, for when so shot, a bison usually lived only five or six minutes. If not successful in reaching a vital spot, the hunter endeavored to ride up along side the wounded animal and push his arrow into its vitals with his feet. The old bows were made of bois d'arc, and while without sinew backing, were very powerful. The strings were of twisted squirrel rawhide. With such bows an arrow was often driven up to the nock in a buffalo.

When plenty of buffalo had been killed, the chief would order out some fifteen or twenty men to hunt alone and bring in meat for the widows and headless families of the tribe. These unfortunates responded by cooking some of the best meat they received and feasting their benefactors. This was repeated until all were provided for, and meat might be seen drying in front of every lodge.

There were generally two chases a day, one just about dawn, and one late in the evening, yet early enough so that the meat could be brought into camp by dark. Hunting was not done in the middle of the day, because the old bulls were then hot and cross and likely to charge.

When every one was plentifully supplied with meat, the Sauk would start back and when four days' journey from their permanent village, the whole party blackened their faces and fasted part of each day, missing their breakfasts so as to be ready to eat vegetable food without further delay when they returned.

The day that the party broke camp on the buffalo hunt, four men were sent back ahead of the rest to report that the tribe was returning. Those who had remained at home would load up their horses with packs of flour, sugar, and lard, and set out to meet the main body. When they met on the prairie these people would measure out a little to each family, so that all would have a taste. All then camped together for a day, after which they all raced home to see if the crops were fit to eat. Then the feast of thanksgiving was held.

That seasonal hunts of this type are of some antiquity with the Sauk is shown by the journal of Peter Pond, writing of the period about 1763[6]. Pond says: "In the fall of ye Year thay Leave thare Huts and Go into the Woods in Quest of Game and Return in the Spring to thare Huts before Planting time."

---

[6]Pond, Ibid, p. 335.

DEER HUNTING

It is not recalled that the Sauk ever hunted deer by night with jacklights placed in canoes. They did, however, make ample use of the wooden deer call which is manipulated in early summer to imitate the cry of a young fawn and thus attract the nearest doe to the spot.

Like the Menomini, the Sauk regard deer calling as dangerous, as wildcats, wolves, and panthers were likely to be lured to the concealed hunter and attack him. It is said that their present Oklahoma habitat was formerly infested with panthers. A Shawnee is said to have been seized by a panther which he attracted by his calls, but that the animal was as frightened as he when it found out its mistake, and fled incontinently.

When hunting, if a Sauk kills a deer, his companion, or anyone coming up to him at that moment skins it, taking all but the head and brisket. If his companion is his father-in-law, he is entitled to take it all.

According to Galland[7], "When one hunter wounds the game and another kills or finds it, and first lays his hands on it, each have a right to his share of the game, i. e., the former takes the skin, the latter the flesh."

When it is to be taken home on a pack saddle, a deer is cut into three pieces with great dexterity. First it is skinned, and then gutted. The belly, from tail root to chin, and including the ends of all the ribs, is cut out and one side is detached, leaving the head and neck on the other. The leg joints are cut, and it is flung over the saddle lengthwise of the horse, a ham and shoulder on each side. The freshly removed skin is thrown over all as a cover, and the hunter may ride home sitting on it. The liver, lungs, and heart are left in the carcass.

When it must be carried on the hunter's back, the deer is gutted, the lower leg bones skinned out and thrown away, and the leg skins tied together, making a natural forehead strap which does not readily untie because the dewclaws which are left on, catch in the knot. The hunter now kneels before a small sapling, works the load on his back, gets the tied leg skins over his forehead, and rises to his feet by pulling himself erect with the sapling.

BEAR HUNTING

Bear were usually pursued only in early fall when there was enough

---

[7]Galland, Dr. Isaac, "The Indian Tribes of the West." The Annals of Iowa, Vol. VII, No. 3, p. 275, Iowa City, 1869.

snow for tracking. When one was located in its den, an adventurous member of the party, relying on Sauk tradition that bears at that season are too inert to attack, would take a rawhide rope, crawl in, tie the bear's forepaw and drag it out, one of their number clubbing it as soon as its head emerged.

At other times bears were attacked on foot, and stabbed with butcher knives before they could rise erect. A bear on his haunches was avoided as being quicker than a man, and, though "left handed," better able to care for himself than an Indian.

When a Sauk is about to kill a bear, he addresses it as *Päshí'to* or "Old Man," or "Old Buffalo," rather than call it by its real name of *Mûkwa*. He then says, "I am going to kill you," and, having thus warned the animal he may fire and it will not be angry, even though painfully wounded.

A HUNTING MEDICINE

The Sauk do not seem to have developed the hunting bundle concept nearly so highly as the Menomini. However Mr. M. R. Harrington has recorded some hunting bundle rituals obtained from the Sauk in his volume on, "Sacred Bundles of the Sac and Fox."

The only article of the kind seen or collected by the present writer is a cap or fillet of otter fur which was regarded as a powerful hunting charm.

FISHING

Undoubtedly when in their ancient homes near the Great Lakes, the Sauk were as maritime in their life as their other Central Algonkian neighbors, but they have today little recollection of the methods of taking fish that they then employed beyond that of sturgeon spearing.

Today the favorite method of fishing is one which they themselves avow that they have learned from the neighboring Creek, since their residence in Oklahoma, the well known water-poisoning method of the Muskhogean tribes of the Gulf states.

A long threadlike root of the bean family called "Devil's shoestring," (*Cracca virginia*) is made into bundles, and taken to good fishing water. Here a stake is driven in the bottom, with a good square top remaining about at the surface. On this the bundles of roots are placed and beaten with a mallet. The exuding juices soon make the water milky in appearance and when from ten to twenty pounds of the stuff have been beaten up, the juice saturates the water of the pool where the current is sluggish, and the fish, numbed and dull, come gasping to the surface. The fishermen now gig them or shoot them with bows and arrows. The work must be done quickly, as the fish usually recover completely within an hour.

An early account of one of the Sauk methods of taking fish while in their ancient Wisconsin forest habitat is given by the Jesuit Father Allouez in his letter concerning the Mission of St. Francois Xavier[8] in 1669-71. He says, "On the 17th, we ascended the River Saint Francois (Fox), which is two, and sometimes three, arpents wide. After proceeding four leagues, we found the village of the Savages called Saky, whose people were beginning a work that well deserves to have its place here. From one bank of the River to the other, they make a barricade by driving down large stakes into two brasses of water, so that there is a kind of bridge over the stream for the fishermen, who, with the help of a small wier, easily catch the sturgeon and every kind of fish, which this dam stops, although the water does not cease to flow between the stakes. They call this contrivance Mitihikan, and it serves them during the Spring and a part of the Summer."

The location of this wier is said by Thwaites to have been at the De Pere rapids of the Fox.

PREPARATION OF ANIMAL FOODS

Venison was usually boiled, as were all small animals, such as raccoons, wood-chucks, squirrels, birds, and fish, for the Sauk, like all Woodland Indians, relished "*napop*," or soup, above all foods. Indian soup, it should be explained, is often a thick stew, composed of odds and ends of everything of animal or vegetable nature in camp, but especially fresh game.

Deer meat was also often cut in collops and spitted on a dogwood wand which was set up obliquely before the fire. In this manner venison was soon dried and could be preserved for some time. It would be eaten as it was, or boiled.

This dried deer meat was often pounded fine in a log mortar of the horizontal style, a type not used by the Sauk for corn grinding, by the way, the vertical form being in favor for that purpose. The pulverized meat was called *noka'hán wias*, and was preserved in woven sacks of bark fiber. When desired for food, it was mixed with tallow flavored with slippery elm bark, and was greatly prized as a delicacy.

For holding this mixture, and for storing lard or tallow, elm bark bowls and mussel shells of large size were used.

---

[8]Jesuit Relations, Thwaites Edition, Vol. 54, p. 217.

Paunch boiling. Buffalo hunters, when without utensils, would remove a bison stomach, clean it, turn it inside out, gather up the ends, and, putting in water, hang it over the fire. Meat was then cut into small dice or cubes, and boiled in this improvised kettle. It is said that the kettle had to be constantly turned so that it would not burn through, and when the meat was done, each in turn drank his share from the natural dish.

Preparation of Fish. Fish were generally boiled, but in olden times, when in the north, tradition has it that they were often dried a little and then smoked. In this condition, they were fit for food, or they could be boiled. No fish have been smoked since the Sauk have lived in Oklahoma.

NAMES OF MAMMALS

Otter	*Kê'totäo*
Mink	*Wi'nêpishkwä°*
Weasel	*Shego's*
Skunk	*Shegák*
Spotted Skunk	*Kêta'gi Shegák*
Beaver	*Omäk^w*
Muskrat	*Asashk^w*
Squirrel	*Hánikwa*
Fox Squirrel	*Sawánik^w*
Gray Squirrel	*Shanigo'*
Ground Squirrel	*Muskotewanîk*
Chipmunk	*Go'weno*
Rat	*Wápikwûno*
Raccoon	*Ä'sêpûn*
Raccoon (small var.)	*Wisa'gäsêpûn*
Opossum	*Aiyê'ni* ("Laugher")
Wildcat	*Pêshiu*
Panther	*Känwasuäo*, ("Long Tail")
Black Bear	*Mûkwa*
Grizzly Bear	*Kagonwî'kishäo* ("Long Claws")
Dog	*A'nêmo*
Wolf	*Muhwä'^w*
Deer	*Pêshigisiwa* or *Pishikisiu*
Doe	*Mätcä'mok*
Young Doe	*Oko'^a*
Buck	*Ya'päo*

Small Spotted Fawn	*Katûkäna*
Fox	*Waku'sha*
Hare	*Mê'shwäo*
Porcupine	*Oká'k^w*
Buffalo	*Nano's*^{wa}

NAMES OF BIRDS

Eagle	*Kê'tiwa*
Crow	*Kakági*^{wa}
Chicken Hawk	*Sikû'ninä^o*
Marsh Hawk	*Mêshkwäkinwä*
Small Red Tail Hawk	*Witcikanupîkwä*
Blue-Jay	*Ti'tiwa*
Goose	*One^{x}k'a*
Swan	*Hähä*^{wa}
Mudhen	*Shäkatä^o*
Loon	*Nishkätäpähûk*
Turkey	*Pänäo*
Blue Heron	*Sa'giwa'*
White Swan	*Asik^w* (Pelican?)
Prairie Chicken	*Mêshisä^o*
Buzzard	*Winákä*
Raven	*Manê'sino Kaka'gi*^{wa} ("War Crow")
Owl	*Witeko^a*
Red Tail Hawk	*Mêskwi'tcito^w*
Duck Hawk	*Käkäk*
Duck	*Shi'ship*
Brant	*Gänê'kihûk*
Helldiver	*Shêkaho*
Wood-duck	*Wikikwä*
Canada Goose	*Onäk^w*
Sandhill Crane	*Wätäpihuk*
Bittern	*Wikû'musi^a*
Quail	*Pokwi*
Partridge	*Pa'kiwa*
Red-headed **Woodpecker**	*Mä'mäo*
Blackbird	*Sû'känak^w*
Curlew	*Muskute' Watuwa'* ("Prairie Shouter")
Mourning Dove	*Manitu Mi'mi*^{wa}
Plover	*Nänê'kinêkwä*

Flicker	*Mêshä'mondo*
Snipe	*Tcinishkᵢʷᵃ*
Prairie Chicken	*Kiwa'ni*
Passenger Pigeon	*Mi'miʷᵃ*
Cardinal	*Mêshkwiwi'shkano'*

NAMES OF REPTILES

Rattlesnake	*Shi hikwä*
Snake	*Mûnitoᵃ*
Snapping Turtle	*Mishikä°*

WEAPONS
CLUBS AND SPEARS

Both the flat and the ball-headed war clubs were formerly used, but the Sauk, in spite of Catlin's pictures, deny that they ever used buffalo hide shields. The bow with flint, bone, or antler-tipped arrows was extensively used in hunting, especially for buffalo in later days, it being considered more suitable for this purpose than the rifle. The custom of shooting fish with the bow and arrow, the Sauk claim to have adopted from the Creek of Oklahoma, from whom they also acquired the custom of poisoning the streams.

The usual war spear or lance had a cedar wood shaft about seven feet long, covered with red list cloth. Scalps were tied on at the point, and it was ornamented throughout its length with feathers and beadwork. Some had handles fourteen feet long, but these were plain. Few of the Woodland Indians used spears or lances, but to this rule the Sauk and the Fox, at least, were exceptions.

War club (generic term)	*k'jîmisi'higun* ("Brain Splasher")
Ball-headed war club	*pêˣkwikiᵘ*
Flat war club	*papû'ke'kiu*
Tomahawk	*papû'kä'hiwît*
War spear	*tcimàgûn*

ARROW POINT MAKING: BOWS AND ARROWS

Flint arrowheads were formerly much used. Two still attached to their shafts (plate XII, figs. 1 and 3, this volume, Part II), and said to be of ancient Sauk make, and from their old home in Wisconsin, were collected. Certainly the flint tips are of true old notched Algonkian style, and made of one of the silexes common on Wisconsin sites. They would not excite comment if found on any prehistoric site of the Wisconsin Algonkians. The shafts, too, bear every indication of age, and, when compared with the ancient antler-tipped arrows described by Willoughby and now in the Peabody Museum of Harvard University, seem authentic. There is therefore no reason to doubt the word of the Sauk from whom they were obtained. With them were several headless arrows equally old. All are feathered with turkey feathers and wrapped with deer sinew. With these arrows came an old bow of bois d' arc, simple, but very powerful, and possessing a twisted string said to be made of squirrel rawhide. It is perhaps the best bow of the very many the writer has seen from the Central tribes. It is said to be contemporary with the arrows, and its appearance bears out this contention.

Plate XII, fig. 2, this volume, Part II, represents another stone-headed arrow. The Sauk who sold it knew nothing of its history, but presumed that the head was an archeological one picked up and re-shafted by the relative who formerly owned it. Its appearance is new, and the wrappings are of stout commercial thread and not sinew.

Billy Harris states that he frequently made antler-tip arrowheads when he was a youth. The antler was boiled in plain water for several hours, the addition of wood ashes being wholly unnecessary, until it softened so that it could be easily whittled into shape. The prongs were detached by girdling and breaking, and a conical opening was made in the porous base for the reception of the naked distal or striking end of the arrowshaft. The gluey substance which had been removed was then replaced, and the shaft thrust in. As it cooled, the joint became very hard and firm and stuck tenaciously to the shaft. When hard once more, it was usually sharpened by grating on a rough stone, such as a block of sandstone.

Arrows were formerly carried in quivers, but no such receptacle can be found in Indian hands today. A fine example of painted rawhide, a conical quiver without fringe, from the Fox, is in the collection made by the late Dr. Wm. Jones in the American Museum of Natural History of New York.

Wm. Harris thought that old Sauk quivers were provided with a special receptacle for the bow, but this is no doubt an error in judgment based on recollections of those seen among the Ioway and neighboring Plains tribes, as all Woodland quivers seen by the writer lack this feature, which is, however, characteristic of the Prairies.

The native names for weapons of this type are:

Bow	*mä^{x}täo*
Headless arrows	*kitákwûnon* ("Naked Arrows")
Wooden (blunt) arrows	*metê^{x}kwûnon*
Deer antler-tipped arrows	*wiwishkûnon*
Quiver	*pito'nwan*

MISCELLANEOUS DATA

MEDICINE DANCE DRUM

It seems probable that the Sauk have lost the art of making their own hollow log drums, since they now take a two gallon wooden keg and stretch a piece of deerskin over it. The corners are twisted tight with a stick, and knots tied in them, with small sticks thrust through so that they will stay.

Two inches of water are left in the bottom, and charcoal is added to the water "to make the drum sound louder." Plate XX, figs. 3 and 4, show old style drumsticks.

Nänä'kwä^a, a flute (plate XXV, fig. 1).

WHITE PAINT FOR LEGGINGS

White clay, called *wabi'wên*, of the same variety that the Kishko moiety uses for paint, is mixed with water until a thoroughly saturated solution is obtained. In this they place a pair of dirty deerskin leggings and thoroughly work them with the hands. They are wrung out, dried, and then worked till soft, the white clay cleaning the leggings and imparting a beautiful white color to them.

ROACHING THE HAIR

In olden times this painful process, called *monágêshäwûg*, or "pulling out the hair," was accomplished as follows: The hair was collected in locks about the thickness of the little finger, and the ends knotted. The warrior or boy was held by his uncles, and his mother or father seized the knots one by one and pulled out the locks by pushing away the victim's head. A standing roach was left from forehead to nape, and this was evened up by grating with mussel shells or burning off with a glowing brand. The bare portion of the head was then painted with vermilion. When a man's hair was growing out again, he was much teased by his joking relatives.

The process of roaching the hair after this manner was looked upon as a very painful one, and the Sauk, like their relatives, the Menomini, declare that the tenderest place was just behind the ears.

ARTICLES USED IN THE MEDICINE DANCE

In plates XXV and XXVI are shown a number of the characteristic articles that form a part of the paraphernalia of the Medicine Dance. In plate XXV, fig. 1, is shown an ancient medicine bag of otterskin, badly worn from use. It has upon the tail an ornament made of the netted quill wrapped thong work, in faded scarlet and yellow, so commonly found on ancient Sauk, Meskwaki, and Ioway specimens. This differs entirely from the woven quillwork of the Menomini, which, like that of the Algonkians and Athapascans north and west of the Great Lakes, involves a closely woven technique of the quills themselves, without a thong foundation.

Fig. 2 of the same plate shows an old otterskin medicine bag with a rosette and line decoration in quillwork applied to the hide of the otter itself, and not to a separate piece of attached deerskin, as is so often the case. Thongs have been brought through the skin of the tail and knotted on the flesh or decorated side, while on the other they hang as attachments for metallic conical jinglers.

Fig. 3, plate XXV, gives an illustration of a very old otterskin medicine bag with quilled foot and tail ornaments attached to pieces of deerskin. The design of this bag is of the open style characteristic of the Menomini, and not at all like the usual Sauk type. The workmanship is, however, much inferior to Menomini work at its best. It is of interest to record that the vendor of this specimen volunteered the information that his ancestors had brought it with them from their ancient home in Wisconsin, and that family tradition stated that it was not of Sauk make, but was obtained from a tribe to the northward, perhaps the Menomini. It was purchased of Aveline Givens.

In plate XXV, fig. 4, is reproduced the likeness of an old otterskin medicine bag obtained from Frank Smith, a Sauk living near Shawnee, Okla., at the time of the sale. It was considered one of the principal bags of a number in his possession, and was made the object of a rather lengthy ceremony on its sale (see Part I of this volume, pp. 47-8). The quilled ornaments in coarse red and yellow work are not attached to the tail of the otterhide directly, but to the feet by means of rectangular pieces of tanned deerskin.

The custom of spirally wrapping the feet of the otters and other animals used as medicine bags, with long strings of braided quills, as among the Ioway and other tribes to the westward, is common among the Sauk, but is not known to the Menomini.

In plate XXVI, figs. 1, 3, and 5, are shown three otterskin medicine bags bearing beaded ornaments. These bags are of respectable antiquity, although not so old as those with the porcupine quill work. A much more modern specimen, that is, an ancient bag with very recent beaded ornaments attached, was obtained, but was not considered worthy of illustration. The design was that of an often repeated swastika, no doubt derived from ideas picked up at some Government boarding school for Indian children, as it is not a native design among the Central Algonkians. However, since 1909, the writer has seen and collected three specimens from the Central tribes bearing this figure; this Sauk bag, a pair of Menomini beaded garters, and a lacrosse bat from a Winnebago. For the last few years the Forest Potawatomi in particular, and to some extent the Menomini, have been incorporating into their beadwork the popular figure of the "Bluebird for happiness" so frequently seen on modern wallpaper and paper napkins.

Plate XXVI, fig. 2, represents a piece of rawhide a few inches square, bound at the ends with red and yellow quill work, and bearing metal tinklers of conical shape with dyed horsehair in their interior. This is one of a pair that were fastened over the instep on the moccasins of members of the Medicine Dance, to make a pleasant sound during the performance of the rites. The writer has obtained similar examples among the Ioway and the Forest Potawatomi.

Figs. 4 and 6 of plate XXVI represent two bundles of invitation sticks used in summoning members to the Medicine Dance, Clan ceremonies, and other rites. The sticks in fig. 4 are cut reeds, in fig. 6 they are sections of cane.

NOTES ON GENS AFFILIATIONS OF INDIVIDUALS

The following brief table of the personal names and gentes of certain individuals among the Oklahoma Sauk with whom the writer had dealings or from whom information was obtained, was gathered in 1923, and is here given as being of some interest.

	English Name	Gens	Native Name or Names	Wife's Gens
1.	Jesse James	Deer	Mamiáshiko, Ugly-Nose	?
2.	Aveline Givens	Deer	Mĕshäĭs, Young-elk Sisiä', White-tail	Fish
3.	Albert Moore	Fox	Sänoä'shkäut, Rattling-brush	Thunder
4.	Frank Smith	born Bear but adopted Thunder	Piä'tcisät, Flying-over	First wife Thunder against old rule Name Po'noä. Present wife, Fish
5.	William Harris	Bear	Mé'siwŭk, Tree-stripped-of-limbs	Ojibway, clan unknown
6.	Tom Brown	Bear	Kwäkwänäpi'kwäo, Winking-eyes	Thunder
7.	Jackson Ellis	Fish	Pémithiä, Stick-in-water	Bear
8.	Isidore Nail	Fish	Kwäkwäpowäo, Floundering-fish	?
9.	Billy Grayeyes	Fish	Ä'pitŭk, Lives-in-water	?
10.	Robt. Davis	Turkey	Nä'po^x, short for 'Péminkĭnä'po^x Lives-in-tree	Kickapoo, gens unknown
11.	?	Turkey	Wapägunäshkŭk, Tracks-in-snow	?
12.	Austen Grant	Wolf	Ä'némiho, Sneaking-off	Washĭshinuk, Appearing-deer daughter of No. 1, Deer gens
13.	James Scott	Wolf	Me^{x}kika^o, Barking-at-you	Thunder
14.	Andrew Conger	Thunder	Ukimawätĕpä, Chief's-head	Deer
15.	Obi Franklin	Bear-potato	Sakijasi^u, Sticking-out	Bear
16.	Henry Hunter	Buffalo	Kishkitäpi^u, Cut-head	Bear
17.	Paul Gauthier	Duck (Menomini descent)	Wigusaka^o, Follows-the-flock	Peoria, gens unknown
18.	?	?	Tukwägi, Fall, or Agona'no	?

EXPLANATION OF PLATE XIII.

PRESENT DAY SAUK LODGE TYPES.

Figure 1. A Sauk square bark house with gable roof, summer type. Near Avery, Oklahoma.

Figure 2. A Sauk round cattail flag wigwam, winter type. Near Avery, Oklahoma.

EXPLANATION OF PLATE XIV.

MEN'S GARMENTS.

Figure 1.   Otter fur hat, with streamer.   Catalog number 30254. Length 5 feet, 2 inches.   Trailer measures 48 inches.

Figure 2.   Warrior's feather headdress.   Catalog number 31466. Length 40 inches.

Figure 3.   Warrior's necklace of grizzly bear claws and otter fur. Obtained from a Fox Indian at Tama, Iowa.   Catalog number 30739.   Length 5 feet, 6½ inches.   The tail or streamer being 4 feet, 4 inches in length.

EXPLANATION OF PLATE XV.

MEN'S GARMENTS.

Figure 1.　Woven bead belt.　Catalog number 30220.　Length without fringe, 32 inches.

Figure 2.　Man's deerskin legging, usual type.　Catalog number 30251b.　Length 32 inches.

Figure 3.　Otter fur garter.　Catalog number 30518a.　Length 29 inches.

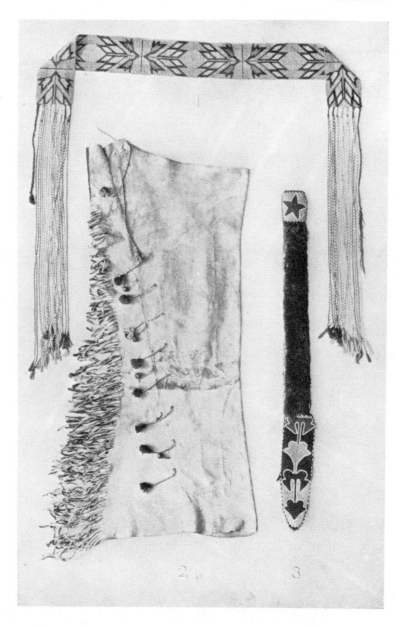

EXPLANATION OF PLATE XVI.

ARTICLES OF APPAREL.

Figures 1, 2, 3, 4, 5, and 9.   Moccasins.   Catalog numbers 30206b, 30207b, 30209b, 30210a, 30211b, 30208b.   Length 10, 10½, 9½, 10, 8½, and 7½ inches, respectively.

Figures 6 and 8.   Quill and horsehair plume shaft ornaments. Catalog numbers 30230, 30229.   Length 9½ and 9 inches.

Figure 7.   Deer hair and turkey bristle roach and antler spreader. Catalog numbers 30742 and 30232.   Length of roach 11 inches, spreader 7⅞ inches.

Figures 10 and 12.   Man's beaded garters.   Catalog numbers 30221 and 30222.   Length without fringe, 12 inches and 11½ inches, respectively.

Figure 11.   Man's breech clout.   Catalog number 30258.   Length, folded as shown, 20½ inches.

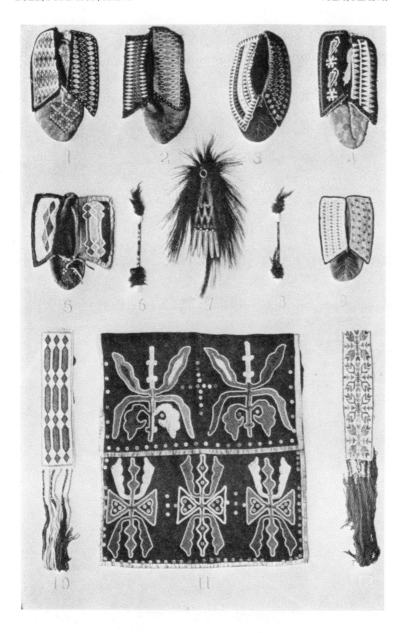

EXPLANATION OF PLATE XVIII.

ARTICLES OF SAUK WOMEN'S DRESS.

Figure 1. Broadcloth robe with silk ribbon applique. Catalog number 30236. Length of vertical ornamental strip 26½ inches.

Figure 2. Woman's knee legging with beaded ornament. Catalog number 30239a. Length 22 inches.

Figure 3. Broadcloth robe with silk ribbon applique. Catalog number 30519. Length of vertical ornamental strip 29 inches.

Figure 4. Woman's knee legging with beaded scroll ornament. Catalog number 30517a. Length 20 inches.

EXPLANATION OF PLATE XIX.

WOMEN'S HAIR ORNAMENTS.

Figure 1.   Hair ornament complete as worn.   Catalog number
            30213a-b.   Length 48½ inches.

Figure 2.   Woven bead tie for hair ornament. Catalog number 30214a.
            Length 10 feet, 9 inches.

Figure 3.   Cloth hair wrapper, with beaded ornament, representing
            human hands.   Catalog number 30212b.   Length 11
            inches.

Figure 4.   Cloth hair wrapper.   Catalog number 30214b.   Length
            12¼ inches.

Figure 5.   Cloth hair wrapper.   Catalog number 30218.   Length 13
            inches.

Figure 6.   Cloth hair wrapper.   Catalog number 30219.   Length
            12¼ inches.

Figure 7.   Cloth hair wrapper.   Catalog number 30217.   Length
            12 inches.

Figure 8.   Hair ornament complete as worn.   Catalog number
            30215a-b.   Length 4 feet, 7 inches.

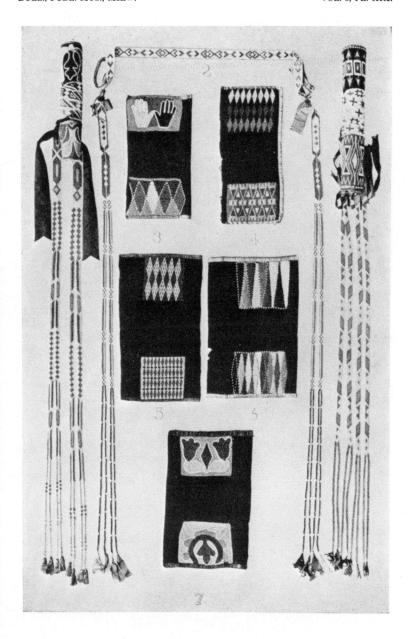

EXPLANATION OF PLATE XX.

MISCELLANEOUS ARTICLES.

Figure 1. Lover's flute, made of cedar. Catalog number 30302. Length 18 inches.

Figure 2. Tobacco pouch. Catalog number 30225. Length 16 inches.

Figure 3. Drumstick from a war bundle. Catalog number 31798. Length 13 inches.

Figure 4. Drumstick from a war bundle. Catalog number 31667. Length 17 inches.

Figure 5. Catlinite pipe, inlaid bowl. Wooden stem with wound bead decoration. Catalog number 30247a-b. Length 23 inches.

Figures 6 - 8. Gourd rattles. Catalog numbers 31461, 30524, 31462. Length 11½, 12, and 11 inches, respectively.

Figure 9. Deer dewclaw rattle, Ioway style. From a war bundle. Catalog number 31799. Length 11 inches.

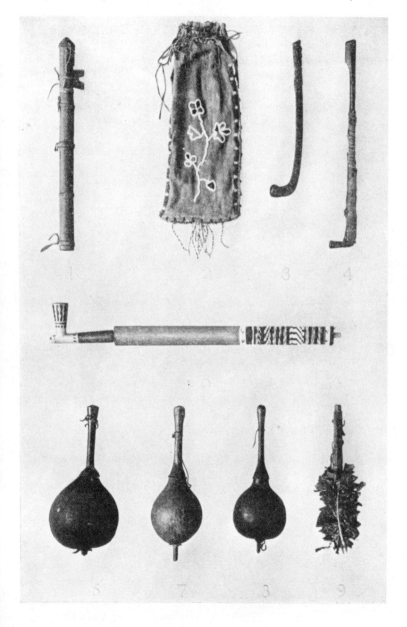

EXPLANATION OF PLATE XXI.

SAUK WOVEN YARN AND FABRIC BAGS.

Figure 1a. Typical yarn bag. Catalog number 30265. Length 20½ inches.

Figure 2a. Bag made of Indian hemp string and blanket ravelings. Catalog number 30261. Length 24 inches.

Figure 3a. Typical yarn bag. Catalog number 30262. Length 21¾ inches.

Figure 4a. Antique bag of basswood bark fibre with designs in yarn of buffalo wool. Catalog number 30260. Length 12 inches.

Figure 5a. Typical yarn bag. Catalog number 30266. Length 18¾ inches.

Figure 6a. Cedar bark fibre bag. Catalog number 30267. Length 21¾ inches.

Figure 7a. Typical yarn bag. Catalog number 30263. Length 20 inches.

Figure 1b. Reverse side of fig. 1a, plate XXI. Catalog number 30265.

Figure 2b. Reverse side of fig. 2a, plate XXI. Catalog number 30261.

Figure 3b. Reverse side of fig. 3a, plate XXI. Catalog number 30262.

Figure 4b. Reverse side of fig. 4a, plate XXI. Catalog number 30260.

Figure 5b. Reverse side of fig. 5a, plate XXI. Catalog number 30266.

Figure 6b. Reverse side of fig. 6a, plate XXI. Catalog number 30267.

Figure 7b. Reverse side of fig. 7a, plate XXI. Catalog number 30263.

EXPLANATION OF PLATE XXII.

HOUSEHOLD UTENSILS.

Figure 1. Pestle. Catalog number 30242b. Length 46 inches.

Figure 2. Large feasting ladle. Catalog number 30280.

Figure 3. Mortar. Catalog number 30242a. Length 22 inches.

Figure 4. Painted rawhide trunk. Catalog number 30526. Length 18 inches.

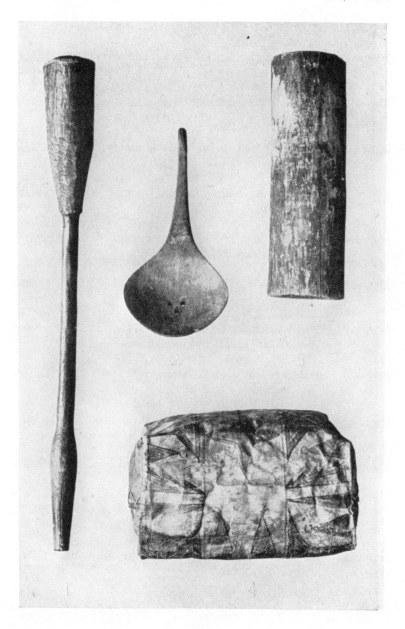

EXPLANATION OF PLATE XXIII.

SAUK WOODEN BOWLS AND LADLES.

Figure 1. Small eating spoon. Catalog number 30288. Length 6½ inches.

Figure 2. Small individual spoon. Catalog number 30290. Length 5 inches.

Figure 3. Small individual spoon. Catalog number 30287. Length 5¾ inches.

Figure 4. Large serving ladle. Catalog number 30281. Length 12½ inches.

Figure 5. Large individual spoon. Effigy handle. Catalog number 30282. Length 11½ inches.

Figure 6. Large individual spoon. Catalog number 30283. Length 10 inches.

Figure 7. Small wooden bowl. Tortoise shell shape. Catalog number 30523. Length 9⅝ inches.

Figure 8. Small wooden bowl. Catalog number 30277. Length 6¾ inches.

Figure 9. Small wooden bowl. Cracked and mended by the Indians. Catalog number 30275. Length 9 inches.

Figure 10. Tiny medicine dose bowl. Catalog number 30278. Length 3½ inches.

Figure 11. Large wooden feasting bowl. Catalog number 30272. Length 17 inches.

Figure 12. Large wooden feasting bowl. Catalog number 30522. Length 17 inches.

EXPLANATION OF PLATE XXIV.

REED MATS.

Figure 1.   Meskwaki effigy mat.

Figure 2.   Sauk mat.   Catalog number 30270.   Length 4 feet, 3 inches.

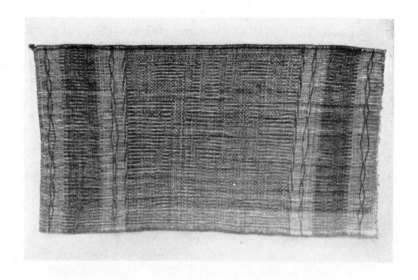

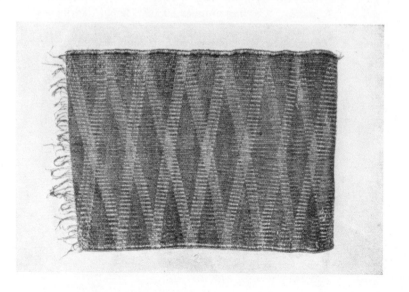

EXPLANATION OF PLATE XXV.

MEDICINE BAGS WITH PORCUPINE QUILL DECORATIONS.

Figure 1.   Otterskin medicine bag with porcupine quillwork ornaments. Catalog number 30751. Length 33 inches.

Figure 2.   Otterskin medicine bag with porcupine quillwork ornaments. Catalog number 30362. Length 30 inches.

Figure 3.   Otterskin medicine bag with porcupine quillwork ornaments. Catalog number 30361. Length 28 inches.

Figure 4.   Otterskin medicine bag with porcupine quillwork ornaments. Catalog number 30360. Length 28 inches.

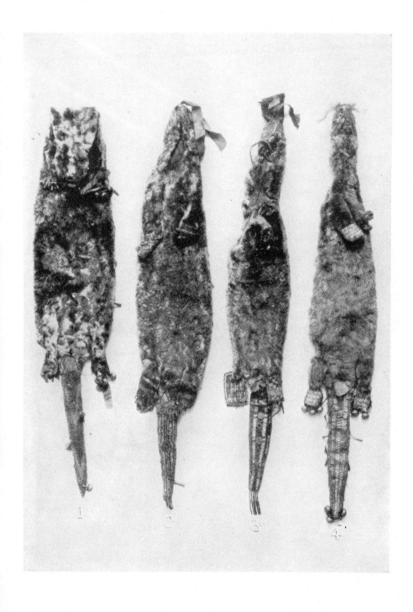

EXPLANATION OF PLATE XXVI.

ARTICLES USED IN THE MEDICINE DANCE.

Figure 1. Otterskin medicine bag. Beaded ornament. Catalog number 30358. Length 3 feet, 11 inches.

Figure 2. Ornament of rawhide with metal jinglers. To be worn on the foot. Catalog number 31685b. Length over all, 5 inches.

Figure 3. Otterskin medicine bag. Beaded ornament. Catalog number 30355. Length 3 feet, 6¾ inches.

Figure 4. Bundle of invitation sticks made of reed. Catalog number 30530. Length 6½ inches.

Figure 5. Otterskin medicine bag. Beaded ornaments. Catalog number 30357. Length 3 feet, 10½ inches.

Figure 6. Bundle of invitation sticks made of cane. Catalog number 30531. Length 10¾ inches.

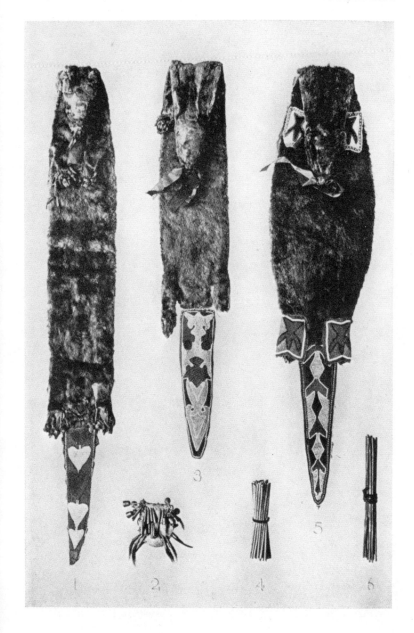